I Can See Tomorrow

I Can See Tomorrow

A Guide for Living with Depression

Patricia L. Owen, Ph.D.

Second Edition

With a foreword by Bert Pepper, M.D.

HAZELDEN®

INFORMATION & EDUCATIONAL SERVICES

Hazelden
Center City, Minnesota 55012-0176

1-800-328-0094
1-651-213-4590 (Fax)
www.hazelden.org

Library of Congress Cataloging-in-Publication Data

Owen, Patricia, 1951–
    I can see tomorrow : a guide for living with depression / Patricia L.Owen ; with a
    foreword by Bert Pepper.—2nd ed.
        p. cm.
    Includes bibliographical references and index.
    ISBN 1-56838-568-4 (pbk.)
    1. Depression, Mental—Popular works. I. Title

RC537 .O94 2000
616.85'27—dc21
                                                            00-044958

Editor's note
The Twelve Steps are reprinted and loosely adapted with permission of Alcoholics
Anonymous World Services, Inc. (AAWS). Permission to reprint and loosely adapt the
Twelve Steps does not mean that AAWS has reviewed or approved the contents of this
publication, or that AAWS necessarily agrees with the views expressed herein. AA is a
program of recovery from alcoholism *only*—use of the Twelve Steps in connection
with programs and activities which are patterned after AA, but which address other
problems, or in any other non-AA context, does not imply otherwise.
    The Twelve Steps for Healing (on pages 239 and 240) are reprinted by permission
of Lewis Andrews.
    All the stories in this book are based on actual experiences. The names and details
have been changed to protect the privacy of the people involved. In some cases, com-
posites have been created.
    This book is not intended as a substitute for the medical advice of physicians. The
reader should consult a physician in matters relating to his or her health.

04 03 02   6 5 4 3

Cover design by David Spohn
Interior design by Wendy Holdman
Typesetting by Stanton Publication Services

Contents

Foreword by Bert Pepper, M.D.   ix
Introduction   1

1. What Is Depression?   7
   What Are the Types of Depression?   7
   Other Ways to Look at Depression   18
   Common Threads of Depression   20
   What If I Am Recovering from Addiction?   22
   What Does This Mean for Me?   30
   Further Questions   31
   What Can I Do to Help Myself?   33

2. Who Has Depression?   35
   You Are Not Alone   35
   What If I Am Recovering from Addiction?   40
   What Does This Mean for Me?   41
   Further Questions   41
   What Can I Do to Help Myself?   42

3. What Causes Depression?   45
   Biological Factors   46
   Environmental Factors   56
   Associated Factors   63
   What If I Am Recovering from Addiction?   78
   What Does This Mean for Me?   79
   Further Questions   80
   What Can I Do to Help Myself?   82

4. Depression and Death   87

The Lethal Connections of Depression   87
What If I Am Recovering from Addiction?   94
What Does This Mean for Me?   95
Further Question   95
What Can I Do to Help Myself?   95

5. What Can I Do about My Depression?
Psychotherapy   97

What Is Psychotherapy?   98
How Do I Find a Therapist?   112
Is Psychotherapy Working? Patterns of
    Change in Therapy   117
What If I Am Recovering from Addiction?   121
What Does This Mean for Me?   122
Further Questions   122
What Can I Do to Help Myself?   125

6. What Can I Do about My Depression? Lifestyle   127
How Can My Lifestyle Affect My Depression?   127
Further Questions   139
What Can I Do to Help Myself?   140

7. What Can I Do about My Depression?
Antidepressant Medication   143

What Is Antidepressant Medication?   144
How Do I Decide Whether to Use Antidepressant
    Medication?   153

What Is It Like to Take Antidepressant
    Medication?   160
What Are the Side Effects of Antidepressant
    Medication?   167
When and How Do I Stop Taking Antidepressant
    Medication?   174
What If I Am Recovering from Addiction?   185
The Effect of Medications on
    Alcoholism/Addiction   197
What Does This Mean for Me?   201
Further Questions   205
What Can I Do to Help Myself?   212

8. *Depression and the Family*   213
    The Importance of Family   214
    What Does This Mean for Me?   220
    Further Questions   221
    What Can I Do to Help Myself?   222

9. *Depression as a Spiritual Phenomenon*   223
    Asking Spiritual Questions   224
    Recognizing When a Spiritual Journey Alone Cannot
        Help Depression   226
    Recognizing the Role of Depression   230
    What If I Am Recovering from Addiction?   239
    What Does This Mean for Me?   245
    Further Questions   246
    What Can I Do to Help Myself?   246

Appendix: A Brief Guide to Common Medications
Used for Depression   *249*
    Selective Serotonin Re-uptake Inhibitors (SSRIs) and
      Other Newer Antidepressants   249
    Unique Antidepressants   252
    Tricyclic Antidepressants   255
    Monoamine Oxidase Inhibitors (MAOIs)   261
    Mood Stabilizers   265

The Twelve Steps of Alcoholics Anonymous   269
Resources   271
Notes   273
Index   289
About the Author   305

Foreword

The mental health field has identified depression as a national and global public health challenge in the past couple of years. The entire field of public health—in the United States, at the United Nations World Health Organization, and in nations around the globe—is measuring depression and its impact on individuals, families, and the global economy.

Depression screenings are now held by many psychiatric organizations in shopping malls across the country, in hope of helping people identify their problem so that they can seek help. The National Institute of Mental Health has undertaken major initiatives to research courses of treatment of depression in children and adults. Tipper Gore, wife of Al Gore, has spoken publicly about her own reactive depression, a response to the serious injuries her son incurred a few years ago. She has promised to make the issue of depression a major concern of her public life.

Five years ago, I had the privilege and pleasure of introducing the first edition of *I Can See Tomorrow*. I was pleased with the book then and knew it could help people who might be depressed sort out some of their problems.

The book was a good map, with clear and simple guide‧posts that help people find their way through the thicket of depression in its many forms.

The second edition has been updated with the most recent, exciting clinical and research contributions to the field of depression. In addition to including current information from clinical and laboratory research on antidepressant medications, Dr. Owen has gone further. She has studied the many ways in which the first edition was perceived and utilized by readers. In this way, she has gained additional knowledge about what a person struggling with depression needs to know, and how they receive and use information from the book. Armed with these additional insights, she has been able to make the second edition even more user friendly than the first.

All of the developments mentioned here, taken together, are helpful because they may reduce the isolation felt by depressed people. Feeling lonely and different are the common symptoms of depression that make it harder for people to seek treatment. The second edition of this book contributes to every reader's understanding of depression and may help them rejoin the mainstream of their family and community.

BERT PEPPER, M.D.

(Bert Pepper, M.D., is founder and executive director of The Information Exchange, Inc., a New York nonprofit organization that gathers and disseminates information on dual disorders.)

Introduction

One of the amazing consequences of writing this book has been learning, in a new and humbling way, of how many people in my life struggle with depression. Pastors and scientists, office workers and writers, students and parents whom I've known casually for years have quietly taken me aside and said, "Hey Pat, I read your book. I'm in the middle of some depression . . ." These are people who get up every day, make a list of things to do, get them done, and more. They are there for other people. They have a sense of humor and a never-ending ability to ruefully laugh at themselves. They're smart and savvy. And yet none of these things provides any sort of protection from the devastating effects of this often invisible disease—depression.

While researching this book, I went to chat rooms and bulletin boards on the Internet and asked specific questions to "real people." I had them answer simple, practical questions such as *How do you get through a bad day? What do your friends and family do that is and isn't helpful? What do you wish they would do? Are you involved in any psychotherapy? What have you learned about yourself from your depression?* Many responses to my questions were very articulate, thoughtful, and heartfelt. One woman wrote, "Sorry, I didn't get back to you right away but I was in the nuthouse (psych humor!)." Another was clearly in the midst of a hypomanic state and wrote pages of lengthy text with no periods or commas. Some wrote of their gratitude of being on the other side of depression. Others shared their unending pain and hopelessness while being in the midst of it even as they wrote. One stands out in my mind among my favorites. A thirty-three-year-old professional wrote:

> *I would like to offer any assistance I might be able to. . . . I think it is very important that people (both those afflicted and those who know and/or love them) learn all they can about this terrible, insidious, life-rotting disease. . . . Believe it or not, a lot of people who suffer from depression don't appear to be any more ill than anyone else, because we learn early that the stigma of mental illness can cause more pain on top of an already unbearable load. . . . "What do YOU have to be depressed about? . . . snap out of it . . . other people are much worse off than you are . . . you're just feeling sorry for yourself . . . everyone gets depressed . . ." This litany goes on and on, one searing dagger after another. Eventually you get tired of trying to explain. You start to pretend you are okay . . . even though you are withering like a dying flower inside.*

Since writing the first edition of this book five years ago, I believe there is a greater awareness and understanding that depression is a real illness. Today, more people are comfortable talking about their antidepressant medication and sharing stories about it. The stigma is still there, but slowly decreasing. People today also have more options. They can use chat rooms on the Internet to talk about their depression anonymously.

If you recognize some signs of depression in yourself, you probably have a lot of questions: *Is it really depression? Who can I talk to about these things? Where can I find help? What's the use anyway?*

By reading this book, you will discover some answers to these questions. As with any serious problem, understanding what's wrong and getting better is not strictly a do-it-yourself project. A sound starting point for your journey is provided here. It's written to help you understand depression and to give you reason to hope.

When you're depressed, it's hard to read and absorb a lot of information. You may find it difficult to concentrate, and your mind may wander. That's okay; if it's important, you'll come back to it. This book is written in a simple, user-friendly format that allows you to dip into it as needed. Most of the chapters include these five main sections:

- Basic information, along with what is known from research or clinical experience. (The appendix offers additional details.)

- *What if I am in recovery from addiction?* This section is written to address the special concerns of people who are recovering from addiction to alcohol or other drugs.

- *What does this mean for me?* This part will help you apply the information to your own situation.

- *Further questions.* Here you will find commonly asked questions and answers about the chapter's topic.

- *What can I do to help myself?* At the end of each chapter, you will find suggested activities and ideas to think about. You may choose to do some or all of the suggested activities right away, or you can come back to them at any time.

Is This Me?

As you read the following examples of how four people struggled with depression, think about yourself. Read the short statements that summarize the concerns illustrated in each person's story. Do you have similar concerns? If so, put a check mark (✓) in the space next to the summary statement. This isn't an exercise to diagnose yourself; it's just to get you started thinking about your own feelings and experiences and how they compare to the feelings and experiences of other people.

❧

Cindi has always been quiet and sensitive. Her feelings are easily hurt, and she is quick to doubt herself. She takes life seriously: when others laugh, she only smiles. She can't remember ever really having fun. For Cindi, life is something to be endured. Recently, she read a newspaper article about someone who was being treated for depression, and now she wonders if she might be depressed too.

"I've never really been happy. Could I be depressed? Others who are being treated for depression don't seem so different from me."

Michael has always been skeptical of counseling and believed that people who went into therapy were weak or just wasting their time. While he has had his share of troubles, he has always handled them by himself. Now he's not so sure he can do that anymore. He feels as though a black cloud is hanging over everything. Nothing is going right and he's cutting himself off from friends. For weeks, his world has steadily been growing bleaker.

"I thought I could always snap out of feeling blue by myself. But I can't seem to shake this sense of gloom."

Everyone who knows Kendra knows her quiet, sure sense of herself. Life always seems to go smoothly for her. Two years ago, however, Kendra's partner in life died. This triggered the resurfacing of lots of unresolved grief from previous losses. When all this grief first hit, she accepted it, knowing deep down that it was time to walk through it. But now, after two years, Kendra feels worn out. Life seems pointless, and she has no energy left to handle all the usual daily problems.

"I've been through many hard times, but now I am experiencing a deep loss (a loved one, health, job). I can't seem to get back on track."

As a young man, Ty was talented, and his future looked bright. But now, in his middle years, he looks back on his life and thinks: *I haven't accomplished anything. I'm stuck in a job that doesn't mean anything to me. Other people have happy families and I don't.* Ty feels more and more hopeless and is planning ways to end his life.

"I feel hopeless and sometimes have thoughts of suicide."

⁓

As these stories illustrate, depression can come in many forms. Whatever form it takes, depression is a very real disease, although it is often invisible to others. But as you will see in the following pages, depression can be understood and treated. Overcoming depression—or learning to live a life with it—is no easy journey; yet, recovery from depression is possible. In this book you will read the stories of actual people who have accomplished this. Learning how they have lived with depression and seeing the choices they have made can open the door to your recovery.

Chapter 1

What Is Depression?

*Just because someone is diagnosed as depressive
doesn't mean they're crazy.*

        ⤙ Kara Ann, age thirty-six, who's experienced
           depression most of her life

Depression is more than feeling blue. It is a condition that
involves the body, mind, spirit, and all the connections in
between. It is often biological, affecting things like appetite,
sleep, and energy level. Depression is psychological, affecting how you feel about yourself. It also affects your social
life, making you want to withdraw from other people.

What Are the Types of Depression?

Depression varies in its intensity. Milder depression is
called *dysthymia*. People with dysthymia can usually continue working and carrying on their daily tasks. But they
have a harder time doing so than most people and don't
enjoy the activity. Major depression, or a *major depressive
episode*, is more severe. It usually prevents people from

going to work regularly and seriously interferes with daily functioning in other ways.

How can you tell if you are depressed? If you were to go to a therapist for an evaluation for depression, the therapist would ask you a series of questions to learn more about you, just as a physician would ask questions and conduct tests to learn whether you had diabetes or heart disease. Depression, as any other illness, has a set of distinct symptoms.

Major Depression

A list of symptoms of major depression is given here.[1] If a person has a major depression, some of these symptoms will have been present for at least two weeks. Before you continue reading, think of how you have been feeling on most days during the past two weeks. Then use this list to start thinking about your situation. Give this exercise some time and thought. Don't try to force a yes if a symptom doesn't really describe your experience. You might want to ask a trusted, observant friend or family member to help you evaluate yourself, especially if you feel unsure that you have a certain symptom. Place a check mark (✓) in front of each symptom you have experienced in the past two weeks.

Cornerstone Symptoms

In the diagnosis of major depression, one or both of the following symptoms are present for at least two weeks:

- *Depressed mood.* I feel down and sad nearly the entire day.

- *Apathy.* I'm not interested in doing the things that used to give me joy or pleasure. When I try to make myself do these things, I lose interest.

Other Typical Symptoms

Staying within the time frame of the last two weeks, which of the following symptoms apply to you?

- *Significant loss of appetite nearly every day.* Nothing tastes good to me. I'm not trying to lose weight, but I've lost quite a bit in a relatively short period of time anyway. I'm just not interested in eating.

- *Having trouble sleeping almost every day.* Often I lie awake for a long time when I go to bed at night. Or, if I fall asleep easily, I wake up during the night for no apparent reason and have trouble going back to sleep. Sometimes I get up at four or five in the morning just because I know I'll never get back to sleep again. This sleep problem doesn't make sense to me. There's no one making noise when I'm trying to sleep, I'm not drinking too much cola or coffee, and I haven't changed my schedule in any significant way.

- *Slow personal tempo.* I feel as if I'm going in slow motion. When I start projects that usually take a short time, I find sometimes that I am not done hours later. I don't know what's happened to the time and why I can't seem to get moving. My friends have noticed that I am moving much more slowly than usual.

- *Fatigue.* I feel exhausted nearly every day. I don't have the energy I used to have to get things done. I feel worn out, tired. Everything is just too much, and getting anything done requires tremendous effort. I can't find any reason for it. I'm not sick that I know of, and I don't have any new demands in life.

- *Feelings of worthlessness or extreme guilt almost every day.* I don't just feel bad when I make a mistake; I feel horrible, as though I'm worthless. I feel like a burden to others. Sometimes the feelings of worthlessness are so strong that I think maybe I don't even deserve to exist. When I read my journal, I see I am writing mostly negative things about myself.

- *A lot of trouble concentrating almost every day.* I have trouble reading a simple magazine article or following the plot of a television show. When I read, I have to start the page over and over again, and still I wonder what I just read. When I try to watch a program, I lose my concentration. I have trouble deciding on simple things, such as what to order at a restaurant. When I meditate, I have trouble letting my mind clear and focus. In the past, I have been able to concentrate.

- *Recurrent thoughts of death or suicide.* I often think it would be better if I were dead. Sometimes I think about ways I could kill myself and even plan ways to do it. Sometimes I don't really put myself into what's going on around me because I think I might be dead soon anyway. I think about how others might react if I were to kill myself.

Atypical Symptoms

Staying within the time frame of the last two weeks, which of the following symptoms apply to you?

- *Fast personal tempo.* I have difficulty sitting still. I jiggle my foot when I'm sitting and move from activity to activity without completing anything. I feel agitated. My friends tell me this is different from my usual pace.

- *Significant increase in appetite nearly every day.* It seems as if I'm eating all the time. But I don't feel full for long, so I'm soon eating again. Or else I eat even when I'm not hungry. I just keep stuffing myself with food.

- *Sleeping too much almost every day.* I'm sleeping much more than usual. I'm always so tired, but I'm not sick. It just feels good to go to bed early and have the day over with. I sleep as late as I can in the morning or nap during the day. Sometimes I wonder if I am sleeping to escape from all my troubles.

Find out whether the symptoms you checked match those of major depression. Place a check mark (✓) next to each item in this list that applies to you.

- One of the cornerstone symptoms is present.
- At least four of the other symptoms are present.

- These symptoms have been present for at least two weeks.
- They are present nearly every day.
- They represent a significant change from the way I usually feel.
- They are not due to another problem, such as a medical illness or the effects of drugs, including drug withdrawal.

If you checked all of the above statements, it is likely that you are experiencing a major depressive episode. If you checked off several but not all of the statements, you may be experiencing a less intense type of depression. People experience depression in many ways. Someone who has an episode of major depression experiences at least one of the cornerstone symptoms of depressed mood or apathy, plus several of the other symptoms described in the preceding section. Often, it is a fairly distinct episode, with a beginning and an end. It may last months or longer.

Depression may vary in its vegetative symptoms. *Vegetative* refers to the biological aspects of depression, such as appetite, sleep, sex drive, and energy level. In *typical depression*, a person loses his or her appetite and consequently experiences weight loss, has trouble sleeping, and has a low energy level. Other people have *atypical depression*, where they experience increased appetite and subsequent weight gain, much more sleep, and agitation. Neither depression is "worse" or "better" than the other in terms of severity. As far as we know, they are simply different biological expressions of the same disease.[2]

Mild Depression (Dysthymia)

Some people find their symptoms do not fit the criteria for major depression, but they recognize that they are not happy and haven't been for a very long time.[3] Their lives are marked by pervasive, unremitting sadness. They may be experiencing a different type of depression called *dysthymia*. It is similar to major depression, but differs in the following ways:

- It is characterized by low mood and at least two of the other symptoms of major depression. In other words, not as many symptoms of depression are present.

- It lasts for a long time, at least two years and sometimes more. In fact, a person may not be able to remember a stretch of time longer than a couple of months when he or she felt free of symptoms and content with life.

- It usually doesn't have a distinct beginning and end. A person may be so accustomed to it that it seems normal.

It used to be thought that dysthymia was simply ingrained in people's personalities—that they were just born unhappy, pessimistic, and withdrawn. In the early 1980s this view began to change, and the field of psychiatry classified dysthymia as *affective*, or a mood disorder. This signaled a change in prognosis: the change occurred because psychiatry began to recognize that people with dysthymia *could* change; they *could* get better.

Depression with Psychotic Features

While most people who experience depression have distorted thinking, a small proportion may have outright delusions or hallucinations. For example, it is common for people with depression to believe they are worthless and that their situation is hopeless. This is *distorted thinking.* *Delusions* are generally even farther afield; for example, one may believe that one's behavior hurts people around the world, or that one's guilt is big enough for a worldwide tribunal. *Hallucinations* are generally auditory. A person who hears voices that comment on his or her life or give advice is experiencing auditory hallucinations. Among elderly people, depression with psychotic features is associated with a worse prognosis. It may take such people longer to get better, or it may be more difficult for them to attain a solid recovery.[4]

Double Depression

Some people who have dysthymia may also experience a major depressive episode. When this happens, they sink even lower than they have become accustomed to. This is referred to as *double depression.* Treatment for the major depression can help these people get back to where they can function again, but they may still feel the low mood and other problems associated with dysthymia. From there they will need to continue working to learn how to live with or reduce their dysthymia symptoms.

The following story of Moses is an example of how dysthymia can gradually grow into a major depression:

I have dealt with depression on and off my whole life. My mom recently said that she thought I was depressed even as a young child. My main symptoms have been feeling like I'm in a black hole with no sign of light. Even with people around, I feel alone. I'm constantly criticizing myself (e.g., too fat, stupid, useless). Nightmares of committing suicide finally got me to the doctor for treatment.

Bipolar Disorder

Depression can be part of a mood disorder called *bipolar*, or *manic-depressive illness*. In this illness, people experience both mania and depression. They may have normal periods in between. Although it's unusual, some people with bipolar disorder have repeated manic episodes with no depression. A small proportion (about 15 percent) of people with bipolar illness are categorized as "rapid cyclers," meaning that they have four or more episodes a year.[5]

Usually, it's the manic phase that alerts other people to the fact that something is wrong. During a manic phase, people feel euphoric or as if they are high. Just as people who are depressed feel overly pessimistic, people in a manic phase feel overly optimistic. Their self-esteem is inflated, and they may become grandiose. For example, they may believe that their ideas will save the world or alter the course of history. Their personal tempo greatly increases; they talk almost nonstop, are easily distracted, and need very little sleep. They may quickly become irritable if they are challenged or crossed. During the depression phase, the person gets no pleasure out of activities. In the manic phase, the person dives into activities excessively, sometimes with harmful consequences. People might do things on impulse, such as suddenly deciding to fly to a faraway place with little or no thought of the daily responsibilities they leave behind. They also might spend all their money on shopping sprees or poorly thought-out investments. A person may also experience a hypomanic state prior to or instead of a full-blown manic state. *Hypomanic* simply means "less than manic." In other words, that person will experience some of the same symptoms in a less extreme form. Whether manic or hypomanic, the person may not be interested in getting help. Annie, who suffers from bipolar illness, wrote me an e-mail one day while in the midst of a manic phase. You can see how disjointed her thought patterns are by her free-flowing statements:

> *Sorry I'm like a little manic today but I like it. At least not the whole experience has been bad I have had some really good times while being sick at least I can laugh at some of the crazy thing I've done while manic. Oh god when I tell my sister and my friends that all laugh with me. Helps a lot. The manic part is great I think sometimes til I crash.*

From her statements, it's apparent that Annie has a sense of humor, is insightful, and knows she needs help. She is especially aware of her need for help during the depressed phase of her illness, but she might be less convinced during a full-blown manic episode. This fits with what clinicians often see when they meet with bipolar patients in a manic phase. People in a manic state may deny that they are ill, and they may see others' attempts to help as demands for conformity.[6]

Seasonal Affective Disorder

One form of depression comes and goes with the seasons. Some people notice that they become particularly depressed during the winter months. This type of depression, which is becoming more understood and gaining more attention by mental health professionals, is called *seasonal affective disorder,* or SAD.[7] (*Affective* in this context means "emotional.") SAD has some distinct features, including

- decreased levels of energy, initiative, or creativity
- increased eating, especially of sweets and starches
- weight gain
- increased sleeping, including naps or sleepiness during the day
- avoidance of friends; decreased socialization

People with SAD often have the other features of depression, such as negative thinking. SAD is much more prevalent among people in northern latitudes, and it is thought to be caused by lack of sunlight. As humans, we are dependent on sunlight to trigger and maintain important neurochemical functioning in our bodies and brains. Some people are especially sensitive to decreases in sunlight, and they develop SAD. Fortunately, symptoms of SAD are quite responsive to treatment with light therapy (see pages 133–134).

Other Ways to Look at Depression

Endogenous Depression

Looking at the way depression arrives—whether it arrives for no apparent reason or in response to an unhappy event—can help you understand it better.

When depression seems to come for no reason, you might wonder what is happening to you. You might feel confused, even alarmed. *Everything was going okay . . . and then out of the blue, I could tell I was getting depressed.* Depression that seems to have no immediate cause is sometimes called *endogenous depression; endogenous* means "birth within." This depression seems to come from within us, not from something that happens to us from the outside.

Mia's story illustrates this kind of depression. She had had periods of sadness during her life, but they had always subsided on their own within a couple of weeks. Then, one time, she found herself experiencing a more serious depression, lasting well into two months.

> *I felt suicidal but had no reason I could pinpoint. . . .*
> *I had many things in my past that would justify being*
> *depressed—violent relationships and so on—but I had*
> *made lots of changes in my lifestyle and worked on my*
> *issues. Then one day I just called the emergency room*
> *at the local hospital and told them something was*
> *wrong but I didn't know what. They told me to come*
> *in for a psychiatric evaluation.*

If you've experienced endogenous depression, you may be frightened because it happened so suddenly, for no apparent reason at all. Once you've escaped it, you may worry that it will return without warning. However, keep in mind that if depression begins to creep back into your life, you may recognize the subtle symptoms leading up to it much sooner and be able to get help earlier on. In addition, as you become more familiar with depression, you may discover ways in which your lifestyle actually contributes to depression or makes you more vulnerable to it. For example, you may not have realized how difficult your job or marriage (or any other situation) was until you were well beyond your first depression. Or maybe you have begun to recognize grief or losses that occurred much earlier in your life that are still affecting you today. Even if the reasons for your depression remain a mystery, you can still get effective treatment and move beyond it.

Reactive Depression

If you know why or when your depression appeared, it is most likely a *reactive depression*. This means that the depression occurred in reaction to something that happened to you.

Ellen recalled the beginning of her depression, when she was in a very difficult situation:

> *I hated the man I worked for and I had a very unhealthy relationship with him. We antagonized each other frequently. He was verbally abusive—and I was paralyzed with fear of losing my job.*

Gabe also knew when his depression began:

When my wife came home and said she wanted a divorce, the bottom just dropped out.

Even if your sadness seems to begin with a specific event in your life, it can turn into a depression that takes on a life of its own. It may begin as the blues, a setback, or a grief reaction, and everyone (including the sufferer) thinks, *This too shall pass.* Often it does. But when it does not, it evolves into a major depression. People with a reactive depression often blame themselves, thinking, *Other people lose their jobs or get divorced, but they get on with their lives. How come I can't just shake off my sad feelings?* What they don't realize is that they have crossed the thin line between a reaction to a tough situation and a major depression. Willpower and reminders to cheer up will not be effective.

The terms *endogenous* and *reactive* might help us understand different ways depression can appear. But depression doesn't always fit neatly into these categories. Many people carry the seeds of depression within them, and the depression only "comes out" during a tragedy or a difficult time in life. There are three other ways depression can be recognized: through anxiety, overcompensation, and isolation.

Common Threads of Depression

Anxiety

Nearly half of all depressed people also experience significant anxiety. Symptoms include worry and obsession, indecisiveness, or social phobia. People may be filled with self-doubt and avoid situations that create uncertainty. These people often have what is called an *external locus of control*. That is, they feel that they have no control over their fate, that it is all up to chance, and that their efforts are of comparatively little use.[8]

Overcompensation

Many people try to overcompensate for the feelings of depression, warding them off by keeping busy. Kaylene tried to bury herself in food. activity, or sleep. She explains:

> *During the time I was experiencing the depressive episodes, I functioned well. I got involved in lots of community activities—a neighborhood recycling project, a fund drive for the preschool. I was busy raising my son, caring for my home, and working. I even began attending law school.*

Isolation

Isolation is also a hallmark of depression. People often begin to avoid friends, skipping meetings or get-togethers they once looked forward to. When friends ask them what's wrong, they are likely to brush them away with superficial comments. Some people use wit or humor to keep others away, even when they are feeling isolated. They often feel intensely ambivalent, wanting to be alone on the one hand but feeling very lonely and unwanted on the other.

What If I Am Recovering from Addiction?

Depression is especially complex when it appears with alcoholism and other addictions. It is probably impossible to go through alcoholism or another addiction without experiencing a tremendous amount of sadness at some point. When an alcoholic or addict feels depressed, many questions arise: *Is it really depression? Am I really alcoholic or am I just drinking to medicate my depression? Do I just feel low because I'm not high on cocaine anymore? Maybe I'm just not working my Twelve Step program in Alcoholics Anonymous well enough. Can I take an antidepressant medication and still be in recovery? Who can I trust to answer these questions?*

It's important to know that depression and addiction can be separate disorders, even if they occur at the same time. In fact, many people experience these two disorders simultaneously. Yet many people do not get the help they need. If you are in recovery and are experiencing a major depression, it's not just a matter of working your program harder—or of giving up on the Twelve Steps altogether. Depression is another problem and requires separate treatment. However, diagnosis and treatment of depression are complicated by addiction. When addicts drink or use drugs, they might feel very unhappy. They might even seek help for their unhappiness. But that help is unlikely to be effective. It's almost impossible to accurately diagnose a depression for people who are active addicts, even if they are honest about their use. Treatment for depression, whether it is medication or counseling or a combination of the two, is likely to have little impact unless the person becomes abstinent from drugs and alcohol.

Even when a person is abstinent and has started along the path of recovery from addiction, diagnosis and treatment of depression can be tricky. Many addicts in early recovery are still reeling from the effects of their addiction. Their lives may be in shambles. Families are confused and alienated, good jobs are lost, and financial and legal consequences are crashing in. On top of this lies the stigma and shame some people feel about coming to terms with their addiction. *Of course I'm depressed! Who wouldn't be?*

Later in recovery, people often struggle with the more subtle repercussions of addiction. They may feel intense sadness. *Now I can see how much of my life has been spent on my addiction. I have years that I need to make up for! And the novelty of recovery has worn off; I'm exhausted and disillusioned.* They may also be learning to deal squarely with the adversities of life without a chemical cushion—and understandably feeling the pain.

For these people, their deep sadness and worry is probably a normal part of the recovery process. They may not have a depression that needs specific treatment. Part of the recovery process will be to experience the pain and move through it without using alcohol or other mood-altering chemicals. In fact, a study done in California on a group of male alcoholics at a Veterans Administration hospital supports this theory. These researchers found that many alcoholics' symptoms of depression decreased dramatically during the first few weeks of recovery.[9] For some people, however, their symptoms are indicative of a clinical depression, and they may need special help from professionals. Read the following section to learn more about this.

Is This Me?

Here are some stories of people in addiction recovery who also experience depression. Each story is followed by a short statement that summarizes the person's concerns. Do you have similar concerns? If so, put a check mark (✓) in the space next to the summary statement. This isn't an exercise to diagnose yourself; it's just to start you thinking about your own feelings and experiences and how they compare to the feelings of other people who have experienced both addiction and depression.

~

Getting into addiction recovery was like coming home for Ben. It felt comfortable and natural. He worked hard applying the Steps to his daily life and was a mainstay at his Alcoholics Anonymous group. Now, out of the blue, he is depressed. In the past, he'd coached many others along who were struggling—he knew how to help them. But now, nothing was working for him.

"I've been in recovery for some time and it's been solid. I've been productive and happy. I'm the type of person who usually enjoys life and people. But suddenly the program doesn't seem to be working for me. I still go through the motions (usually), but I'm getting worried. I don't understand what's happening to me. Is it that the program isn't working anymore?"

Cara was beginning to realize that she has been depressed since she was a little girl. When she was an

adolescent, her depression came out as rebellious-
ness and sullenness. She was alienated from others
and escaped into drugs. Now, twenty years later, she
is drug and alcohol free, and her life is settling down.
She has continued to attend Alcoholics Anonymous
meetings. However, she still feels down a lot of the
time. She credits Alcoholics Anonymous and therapy for keeping her alive, but she wonders why she's
still feeling depressed.

*"I remember being depressed long before I started hav-
ing a problem with alcohol and other drugs. In fact, I
think I used alcohol and other drugs to medicate my
sadness and painful feelings. I'm in recovery now. But
I wonder, was my problem really addiction or was it
depression? I still feel depressed."*

Levi finally agreed to accept help with his drinking.
No one would listen to him anyway when he tried
to tell them, "I drink because I'm depressed. If you
had my life, you'd drink too." Now he realizes he
was being defensive and denying his drinking problem. His life was not a happy one, with or without
alcohol.

*"I'm new to recovery and I think I'm depressed. I'm
working on my alcohol problem, but I don't think my
depression is getting better."*

&

How Is Depression Related to Addiction?

Depression complicates addiction and addiction complicates depression. People who are struggling with both often wonder, *Is it really two disorders or does it just seem like it?* Many people do have two disorders—both addiction and depression—but other people experience a depression that is directly related to their addiction.

Some people claim that they used alcohol or other drugs because they were depressed or, conversely, that they became depressed because of their addiction. These aren't just excuses; they may be picking up on a subtle pattern.[10] Research on the relationship between alcoholism and depression has found that for most alcoholic men, the alcoholism comes first, and the depression develops later. For most alcoholic women who are depressed, the opposite is true: the depression develops first, then the alcoholism.[11] But regardless of the order, people who are addicted will need treatment for that; overcoming depression, in itself, will not cure addiction. In the same way, overcoming addiction will not necessarily cure depression; people in addiction recovery who are also depressed will often need treatment for the depression too. And since most people have a hard enough time accepting one disorder, having to come to grips with a diagnosis of both depression and addiction can seem especially unfair.

People who experience their first episode of depression before they develop an addiction have what is known as *primary depression*. In this case, *primary* doesn't mean "most important"; it means "first" or "on its own." If a person is experiencing a clear primary depression, it's more likely the depression will need its own treatment. In fact, if left untreated, depression can contribute to relapses and difficulties in getting a strong foothold in recovery from addiction.

Mary's story is an example of primary depression. She remembers being unhappy and dissatisfied as a child for no apparent reason. By adolescence, she was experiencing friction with her parents and had started drinking and taking drugs. (Depression often appears as rebellion during adolescence.) As the years went on, she continued to drink and use drugs, and she attempted suicide numerous times. Finally, she received treatment for chemical dependency, got into stable recovery, surrounded herself with loving people, and found a job she liked.

> *My recovery from addiction was amazing to me. I felt better quickly, and my life became better. I was active in Alcoholics Anonymous. I attended daily meetings, I was active in service, I found and developed a relationship with a sponsor, and I sponsored other people. I was able to complete a bachelor's degree, get married, and have a child. I practiced the Twelve Steps and discovered a spirituality I had always sought and, like the Big Book says, my entire attitude and outlook on life changed. On the surface, things looked great. But I wasn't sure much had changed on the emotional level. I still experienced random deep depressions that came without any apparent trigger.*

Depression is also called primary if it begins when a person has been abstinent from alcohol and other drugs for at least six months. (Remember that primary means that the depression occurs on its own and not as a direct consequence of addiction.) This is what happened to Larry three years into his recovery:

I began to doubt the power of the program and the changes I'd made because of it. I don't know just how the gray curtain came down on me, but it seemed that as hard as I was working with my recovery from alcoholism, I should be much more "joyous and free" and experiencing the "freedom from bondage" that I kept witnessing in the program. I didn't feel this way at all. I felt cynical, lonely, and hopeless. I even thought of killing myself—that's not like me at all.

Larry was doing everything right, but he knew something was missing. He had the experience of being in a solid program of recovery from addiction, doing well for a long time, and then experiencing depression. In his case, the depression seemed unrelated to his alcohol addiction.

If the depression occurs after a person has started using or drinking, it's called a *secondary depression. Secondary* doesn't mean "of secondary importance"; it means "it occurred second," or that it is related to the alcohol or drug use. Secondary depression might stem from the growing feelings of futility in trying to control alcohol or drug use, or from facing the pain of all the mounting consequences of addiction. Most people with secondary depression find that their feelings of depression subside in just a few weeks as they stay abstinent and start a new life. In other words, as abstinence grows stronger, the depression lessens. Darrell wasn't depressed before he started drinking. He had had the normal ups and downs that everyone has, but he was always able to shake them off. This was different: Darrell experienced a secondary depression.

When I went into treatment, I was devastated. I thought my problem with alcohol was my own business. Now everyone knew it. I felt ashamed and guilty. I felt like I let everyone down, most of all myself.

Looking back, Darrell realized that when he started depending on alcohol, his world got smaller, and he began to lose his happiness. Staff at the treatment center talked to Darrell about his depression and suggested that he allow himself more time in recovery before deciding whether to pursue treatment for depression. The staff told him his depression might resolve itself with abstinence and a solid recovery program. Darrell did experience fewer and fewer symptoms of depression as he progressed in his recovery from addiction.

Most people have trouble objectively untangling their own stories of depression and addiction. It's especially important for people in early addiction recovery to find a therapist to talk to about their depression. Getting a good assessment can help make recovery from depression possible.

And remember that the picture is not entirely bleak. People who are recovering from addiction may have special advantages in dealing with depression. They have already overcome adversity in dealing with their addiction and have developed strengths because of that. There are other stories throughout this book that show how people in recovery from addiction have found help for their depression.

What Does This Mean for Me?

Some people think depression is synonymous with feeling blue. After a bad day at work or an argument with a friend, they might moan, *I'm so depressed!* What they really mean is that they are sad, unhappy, discouraged, or frustrated. This casual use of the word *depression* is unfortunate because it can trivialize the state of true depression. Depression is a serious disorder. According to the Centers for Disease Control, in 1997 more than thirty thousand people in the United States killed themselves,[12] and for most, untreated depression was the reason. There is hope for people with depression, but first, they need to know that it's not something they can just snap out of.

The difference between feeling down and being depressed is like the difference between having too much to drink one night and being an alcoholic. Someone who is not an alcoholic and drinks too much one night can wake up the next morning and say: *Whoa! I overdid it last night. I'm not going to do that again!* And, not being an alcoholic, the person will probably have no further problems with alcohol. But everyone knows what happens when alcoholics say that. Maybe they will be able to quit drinking for a while or carefully control their intake. But if they are alcoholic, just deciding not to drink too much will not solve the problem. In time, they'll have another drinking episode. It is not their fault or necessarily something they want. But until they understand that they are alcoholic, and what that really means, they will remain stuck in the same cycle.

It's the same with people who are simply feeling blue. Someone who is not truly depressed but is in a low spot can say: *Hey! I'm getting gloomy. I'd better lighten up here! I think I'll go out and do something fun and try not to let my troubles get to me.* People who are not truly depressed can probably do just that. But for those experiencing a major depression, the best they may be able to do is act or bury their symptoms in busyness. Over time, the depressive symptoms will reappear, and the person will become even more self-blaming and discouraged. As with the people who don't recognize their own alcoholism, these people will remain stuck until they understand they have depression.

This chapter has looked at different types of depression, a long list of symptoms, and a variety of ways that depression presents itself. In the following chapters, we'll be looking at the ways depression affects not only feelings, but the body and mind as well.

Further Questions

I don't exactly fit the description of depression. Does this mean I should just try to forget about it?

No, not at all. Your feelings and your situation are just as serious as anyone's and need just as much attention. There is some research that indicates that even having some symptoms of depression may be a precursor to more serious depression later on.[13] If you are experiencing any of the symptoms described in this chapter, it means that something is going on inside you. Getting a thorough assessment by a professional is a good place to start. And even if you are not diagnosed as having a major depression, it's still important to take care of yourself and continue to explore the path you are on. Emotional pain is difficult, no matter what the label is.

Does it matter what kind of depression I have?

Knowing the variations of depression can help you see that you are not alone. There are different types of depression, and not everyone fits a mold. Some people think, *I'm not feeling like so-and-so did when she was diagnosed with depression, so I must not really be depressed. Whatever I am experiencing must be something different.* Two people can be depressed but have different symptoms.

Learning about all the ways that depression can express itself can also give you more ideas about how to help yourself. There are many things you can try on your own. Some ideas may come from reading this book.

If your depression doesn't begin to clear even as you make changes in your life and try new things, you might need help from a professional. This does not mean your efforts have failed. Rather, a thorough assessment by a skilled, experienced, mental health professional—one who has seen hundreds of people with varying degrees of depression, during all phases of the illness—can give you more information to work with. Professionals have a perspective that can help you see yourself in ways that you cannot see on your own.

What Can I Do to Help Myself?

When you're feeling depressed, you may start to wonder, *Where can I even begin?* Here are some small first steps you can take to help yourself.

1. Have you completed the exercise in this chapter (pages 8–12) to assess your symptoms of depression? If not, this might be a good time to do so.

2. If you're concerned about your symptoms of depression, who can you talk to? If you have friends or family members who would understand and be good listeners, this might be the time to talk to them. Showing them the checklist you filled out can be a good discussion starting point.

3. Do you feel you need a professional assessment to learn more about yourself and your feelings? Could you call a mental health center to make an appointment? The information in chapter 5 can give you more guidance in how to find what you need.

4. Maybe you are already seeing a therapist for other issues. Have you talked about your symptoms of depression with him or her? Now that you understand what the symptoms are and have names for them, perhaps you'll feel more able to do so.

5. Listen to other people talk about themselves. Do you know some people who say they are

struggling with depression? In the past, perhaps you haven't noticed that friends or acquaintances were acting depressed. Perhaps you haven't paid full attention to them. But now you know more about what they may be experiencing. Could you ask them about their depression? Listening to them can (a) help validate their experience; (b) help you learn more about depression; and (c) perhaps help you get a clearer picture of what is going on inside you.

For people in addiction recovery: Is there a mental health professional in your community who understands both chemical dependency and depression? You might need to ask around in the recovering community to get some names.

Chapter 2

Who Has Depression?

You Are Not Alone

If you're depressed, you might feel alone and think that no-body could understand the depth of your pain. You might be embarrassed or ashamed about your feelings and think that others would look down on you if they knew how you felt. The fact is, you have company. Many well-known people have spoken or written about their depression so that their stories might give strength and hope to others. Art Buchwald, the Pulitzer Prize–winning writer and humorist gave a talk at Emory University in 1999 about his periodic battle with depression, saying, "It's a terrifying phenomenon." Kathy Cronkite, accomplished writer, journalist, public speaker, mental health advocate, and daughter of news journalist Walter Cronkite, wrote an excellent first-person account of her depression, describing depression as "the loneliest illness there is."[1]

Mark Rothko (1903–1970), champion of the American abstract expressionism art movement, whose vibrant, color-filled works were shown in every prominent museum in Europe and America, suffered from depression and committed suicide. William Styron, author of *Sophie's Choice* and other novels, said of his illness, "The ferocious inwardness of the pain produced an immense distraction that prevented my articulating words beyond a hoarse murmur; I sensed myself turning wall-eyed, monosyllabic, and also I sensed my . . . friends becoming uneasily aware of my predicament."[2] Dick Cavett, the engaging, quick-witted top talk-show host has experienced crippling periodic bouts of depression since his freshman year at Yale. Neither he nor those around him understood what was happening to him, and he did not get help until decades later. But during episodes of depression, he carried on with his career, as one journalist wrote: "Mr. Cavett did do a series of talk shows for public television during this time, but he said they were torture because of his lack of concentration. He generally wasn't sure that he was asking his guests relevant, interesting questions. He felt 100 times worse than he looked to others, so the show came out satisfactorily."[3] Judy Collins, one of the leading female singers to emerge from America's folk revival in the early 1960s, has written an artful, moving account of her son's alcoholism, depression, and ultimate suicide. From her own journey, she is able to understand his, and move through the pain to continue and grow her own life.[4]

These are just a few of the well-known people who have lived with depression. No doubt others come to mind for you, and you may know several people among your family and friends who have also talked openly about their depression. Depression is so prevalent that it has been called the "common cold" of mental illness. At least twenty million people in the United States experience depression every year. Estimates vary widely, but a major survey of the U.S. population found that 17 percent of adults experience a major depressive episode at least once in their lives. Another 6 percent have experienced, or will experience, dysthymia (the type of low-level, chronic depression that usually starts when a person is young). About 2 percent of the general population have or will experience a bipolar disorder (the type of depressive disorder that varies from one extreme to the other—being manic during some periods of time and very depressed at other times, or having episodes of mania without depression). Looking at all types of depression, a large number of the population of the United States—about one-fifth of all adults—can expect to experience some type of depression in their lifetime.[5]

While both men and women are vulnerable to depression, the rates are higher among women. About twice as many women as men experience a major depressive episode (as well as dysthymia) in their lifetime. Surprisingly, though, the rates of manic-depressive illness among men and women are about equal.[6] Women with small children have among the highest rates of depression.[7] Low-income mothers who have a place to live and homeless mothers have rates of depression double that of women in the general population.[8]

There is also more depression among both men and women at the lowest income levels.[9] People living in poverty may be more vulnerable to depression because they may become discouraged and disheartened by their situation and then develop clinical depression. It may also be that some people at higher income levels become less able to function when they get depressed and, therefore, lose their jobs and move into lower income levels.

Even though depression is more common among some populations, it can and does strike people in all walks of life.

People of Any Ethnic Background Can Become Depressed

Although people of all colors and races can become depressed, rates of depression are generally found to be somewhat higher among Latinos than whites. Overall, blacks have lower rates, but one large national survey found that the highest lifetime rate of depression was among black females between the ages of thirty-five and forty-four years.[10] Surprisingly, the large difference in depression between men and women may be unique to North American Caucasians, and not necessarily true in other populations. One large population survey of Chinese Americans in Los Angeles found that both men and women had about the same rate of depression. In both cases, it was a low rate (7 percent), less than half of the rate found in the general population. However, with increased acculturation, they found that the rate in Chinese American women rose significantly. So it may be that Western ways or fitting into the American culture may be especially difficult for this population of women. Other researchers have found no gender differences in other groups, including African Americans in Maryland, Southeast Asian refugees in Canada, and Korean Americans in Chicago. A large U.S. population survey study found that Jewish men had the same high rate of depression as Jewish women; in other religious subgroups, there were no gender differences.[11]

People of All Different Educational Backgrounds Can Become Depressed

People who have an advanced college degree are just as likely to become depressed as those who have not graduated from high school.[12]

People of Any Age Can Become Depressed

Some studies show that the likelihood of becoming depressed is higher among younger people and wanes a bit with older age.[13] But it's a myth that young people are in the best years of their lives because "they have everything to look forward to" or that older people should be immune to depression because they are in their "golden years" and past the demands of careers and growing families. Each age has its own challenges.

Older adults are more likely to express their depression through somatic complaints—that they don't feel well physically—and they are less likely to seek help for their depression.[14]

People in Marriages and Those Who Are Alone Can Both Become Depressed

Depressed people who are unattached—separated, divorced, widowed, or never married—sometimes think, *If I were in a relationship, I wouldn't be so depressed.* There is some evidence to bear this out.[15] But this is not a simple cause-and-effect situation. Depression prevents some people from entering into intimate relationships or destroys the relationships they have built. For others, the loneliness of being single sets the stage for depression. Regardless, both attached and single people are vulnerable to depression. The real factor is not whether a person is in a relationship, but the quality of the relationship. This will be covered more in chapter 8.

People in All Sorts of Careers Can Become Depressed

Having a stable, prestigious, or well-paying job doesn't protect a person from depression. And all types of companies are increasingly recognizing that many of their employees are depressed. Companies care about this for humanitarian reasons, but they also know that depression among employees affects the bottom line. Depression increases absenteeism and decreases productivity. In other words, even when depressed people make the (often monumental) effort to be on the job, their ability to work efficiently may be decreased. We also know that general medical costs for depressed people are about one-and-a-half times higher than they are for nondepressed people.[16] Studies have shown that treatment for depression dramatically decreases health care costs.[17]

What If I Am Recovering from Addiction?

People with addiction are much more likely to experience depression in their lifetime than people without addiction.

While the numbers vary greatly, many research studies find that the rate of depression among alcoholics is about two to three times higher than in the general population. And for those who have been dependent on both alcohol and other drugs, the likelihood of depression is even higher— about 10 percent higher.[18] Manic-depressive illness has an especially high correlation with addiction. More than half of the people with a manic-depressive illness have a drug or alcohol problem.

What Does This Mean for Me?

In short, depression can happen to anyone. And it happens to tens of thousands of people every year. It happens to people with high incomes, low incomes, men, women, people of all races, and to the young and old. Being depressed is not a sign of moral weakness, lack of intelligence, or incompetence. If you experience depression, it is not your fault and it is not something to be ashamed of. There is help available to you.

Further Questions

Why do the statistics about who has depression matter to me?
Just this: they mean you are not alone. This is not your own private hell. What you are experiencing is something that others have experienced too. And many of them have not only survived, but also have come out the other side. Because so many people have experienced depression, employers and society in general are recognizing it. Depression is losing its stigma. More and more, people understand

that overcoming depression is not a matter of "cheering up" and "counting your blessings." More people understand that depression strikes people from all walks of life: ambitious and successful people; sensitive and giving people; rich and poor people; people with high and low IQs; tough and soft people. If you are experiencing any type of depression, you do not need to be ashamed or apologetic.

I hear and read more about depression now than I did in the past. Is depression increasing or are people just talking about it more?

Depression has always been a significant problem, but it is becoming more visible because people are acknowledging it. More and more people see that it can be treated successfully. Most people with a depressive disorder can find a treatment method that works. It is tragic that anyone would suffer alone and without help when so much is known about how to treat depression.

What Can I Do to Help Myself?

Even though depression is widely recognized today as an illness that can strike anyone, many people still feel some shame about it. Do you feel shame about experiencing depression? Perhaps it would help if you could *really* give yourself permission to believe that anyone could experience depression. To help yourself understand this fact on a personal level, try the following action steps.

1. Have you thought you were the only one with depression? Imagine a room full of one hundred

people. In your mind, count off twenty of them: these people have known depression too. (*For people in addiction recovery:* Imagine walking into a large, open Alcoholics Anonymous meeting of one hundred people. In your mind, count off thirty of them: these people have experienced depression similar to yours. Let yourself sit with this for a while.) If you fully take this in, you may find yourself able to be more compassionate with yourself and others. Even though the world can look like it is filled with busy, happy, productive human beings, you are not alone in your suffering.

2. Some people who are doing very well in life now have experienced depression in the past. You might not know it to look at them. Whom could you interview to find out if they have experienced depression? A friend? A family member? Someone in a recovery support group? Could you ask the question of your whole recovery group? This exercise may surprise you. You may find that a very active and lively person has experienced depression in the past. As you do the exercise, remember that you do not have to talk about your own experience if you don't want to.

Chapter 3

What Causes Depression?

I feel that a combination of genetics and a poor childhood is my reason for depression.

~ Angela

Depression is a mystery. Some people can live most of their lives free from depression and then get caught in its grip. Other people battle it their whole lives. Still others go through life without ever experiencing depression. This illness has probably existed since the beginning of time; it has been heavily researched, and still we do not know its cause. A great deal of research has been aimed at developing new medications, and it's from that work that we are able to make some inferences about what causes depression. And, on a different front, we are making progress in understanding the biochemical connection between mind and body, behavior and mood, and from this we are also understanding how events in our daily lives may actually affect the chemicals in our brain.

Most likely, depression is many disorders, not just one. Consider the term *fever*. At one time, it was thought that fever was an illness unto itself. Today, it's known that fevers are caused by many different illnesses and conditions. Some fevers are caused by chicken pox, some by pneumonia, and some are due to blood poisoning from a cut. Having a fever is a sign that something is wrong. Similarly, depression is a sign that something is wrong—physically, spiritually, or emotionally. And regardless of how the depression gets started, our whole being is affected. Current theories stress the biological and chemical nature of depression, and that is where we will begin.

Biological Factors

Genes

If you are experiencing depression, you might be able to look back at your family—grandparents, parents, siblings—and see that you're not the first one in your family to experience it. Depression often runs in families. In fact, some families have a rate of depression that is two to three times higher than the rate in the general population.[1] This is true for all types of depression, but especially for bipolar disorder, the type of depression that is characterized by extreme swings between depression and mania. A person who has bipolar disorder probably has relatives with the disorder and other forms of depression. Because of these strong patterns, one theory is that depression is carried in the genes, in the chemical makeup passed down to us from our parents.

But just because depression runs in families does not necessarily mean it is genetic. It could mean that the family environment creates a climate ripe for depression. For example, when parents are depressed, they probably cannot convey to their children the love and warmth they would if they weren't depressed. In turn, the children may become more vulnerable to depression. Or the children may subtly take on the negative beliefs of a depressed parent. So how can we know whether a disorder like depression is caused by genes or by the mood of the family?

Researchers do special studies of families to test out these theories. Family studies can get quite complicated because there are so many factors involved. But let's take a short detour to understand how these special studies are done.

Twin studies are one of the most fascinating types of studies. Twins are either identical or fraternal. If they are identical, they share all their genes. If they are fraternal, they share about half of their genes, just like any two siblings. In either case, they usually grow up in the same family. If depression is carried in genes, identical twins should always be exactly concordant for depression. This means that if one twin is depressed, the other one should be, too, because they have exactly the same genetic makeup. On the other hand, if depression is caused by the environment—by the way a person is raised or the mood in the family—the rates of depression in identical twins and fraternal twins should be pretty similar.

Are identical twins equally depressed? No. But there's enough similarity in their rates to give researchers hope that they are on the right track. Studies vary quite a bit; depending on the study, the concordance rate for identical twins ranges from 33 to 70 percent,[2] though typically between 40 and 44 percent.[3] In other words, about half the time, if one identical twin is depressed, the other identical twin will be too. The concordance rate is higher for mania; if one identical twin has experienced a manic episode, there is an 80 percent chance that the other identical twin has too. You might think, *Well, that's only natural; twins are so emotionally and physically close to each other.* That's where comparisons come in. Fraternal twins' concordance rate for depression is only 20 percent. This rate is a bit higher than the general population rate, but far less than that of identical twins. If depression was caused just by the environment—the way the family operates—fraternal twins should have the same rates of depression. But they don't. Therefore, it's likely that something in the genes is making a difference. It's interesting to note that several studies have found that the genetic contribution for women is more than it is for men. For example, in one large population study of twins in Australia, researchers found that the concordance for severe depression among monozygotic females (those who have come from a single egg) was high, 50 percent; but among men in the sample, the concordance rate was much lower, only 34 percent. Severe depression was measured because this typically shows greater heritability, or chance of being inherited.[4] In other words, for reasons we do not understand, it may be that women are more susceptible to developing depression in response to genetic factors than men are.

Another way to research how genes affect depression is to compare adopted children and biological children.[5] If depression is primarily genetic, then the biological children of depressed parents should have a higher rate of depression than other people, regardless of how healthy their home life is. Researchers studied a group of depressed adults who were all adopted at a very young age. They interviewed and examined records of these people's biological parents and adoptive parents. The researchers found that the adoptive parents, the parents they grew up with, had a rate of depression that was about the same as for the general population—about 12 percent were depressed. But when the researchers went back to the biological parents, they found almost three times more depression. The suicide rate among their biological relatives was even higher. In their depression, the group of depressed, adopted adults were more like their biological parents than their adoptive parents. This suggests that their genes influenced their depression. (These researchers also studied adopted people whose biological parents were *not* depressed. They didn't find higher rates of depression in this group. Being adopted, in itself, doesn't seem to make a person more prone to depression.)

If depression is genetic, what exactly might the genes be carrying? Genes carry small bundles of information. It is unlikely that they can carry the whole story of depression. Instead, they might carry information about resiliency to stress, perception of rejection, sensitivity to emotional pain, or ability to experience joy and pleasure. Many of these states can be regulated or affected by brain chemicals. So genetic makeup may lay down the biological structures that alter brain chemistry and make people more or less vulnerable to the characteristics that add up to depression.

Genetic studies of depression show that people carry something in their genes that may make a difference in whether or not they develop depression. This is especially true for bipolar disorder. It might be that different forms of depression have different genetic strength. Just as important, genetic studies show that something besides genetic makeup contributes to the tendency to become depressed. If depression were passed down the generations as clearly as eye color or body build, identical twins would have exactly the same depression experiences. It is clear from twin studies that this is just not true. Something else is also contributing to depression.

Brain Chemistry

The promising theory of depression is that some people who are depressed have imbalances of important chemicals in the brain, called *neurotransmitters*. Neurotransmitters carry messages between the nerve cells in the brain. They begin in one cell, go out into an open space between the cells (a *synapse*), and then move into another cell. During this journey through the brain, neurotransmitters carry important signals about the need for food and sleep and people's basic mood states. In depression, these messages break down. Brain cells on both sides of the synapse are oversensitive or insensitive, which in turn creates a deficiency of a particular kind of neurotransmitter. In depression, the two types of neurotransmitters that are thought to be most affected are *serotonin* and *norepinephrine*.

There is no way to measure levels of neurotransmitters in living human beings. Nothing in the brain holds still long enough to study it; chemicals and electrical impulses swarm throughout it. And the brain is so well protected that it can only be studied indirectly. Because the levels of neurotransmitters can't be measured as they flow through the brain, some inferences have to be made. For example, it is known that medications that affect neurotransmitters also affect depression. So if antidepressants improve depression, and they also affect the level of neurotransmitters, it's likely that neurotransmitters play an important role in depression. In fact, as we shall see in later sections, researchers developing new medications to treat depression focus on medications that increase levels of serotonin or norepinephrine.

A current evolving and promising theory of depression is that a certain part of the brain, called the *hypothalamic-pituitary-adrenal axis* (or HPA axis) is overactive in depressed people and produces certain hormones that, in turn, produce symptoms of depression.[6] There is growing evidence for this view of depression. First we'll take a look at the mechanics of this theory, and then we'll see why it may be so important in understanding depression.

The HPA axis is integrally involved in what's known as the "flight or fight" response, a primitive but still very active chain reaction that occurs in the human brain when an emotional or physical threat is detected. Here's what happens:

- Something stressful occurs that signals to the body that survival is threatened. For an infant, it might be abuse or neglect. For an adult, it might be a burglar breaking into the house or a loved one unexpectedly announcing that he or she is leaving. Even if an adult uses logic to reduce the fear or pain, the initial emotional response takes precedence.

- The body prepares to deal with the threat—
  either to stay and fight or to run away. It does
  this in an amazingly elegant and complex way.
  Simply put, a part of the brain called the hypothalamus increases a chemical (CRF) that sends
  a signal to another part of the brain, called the pituitary gland, telling it to increase the production
  of another chemical (ACTH). The ACTH zooms
  down to the adrenal glands on top of the kidneys,
  to quickly produce more of another chemical,
  called *cortisol.*

- Each of these natural chemicals in the body plays
  an important role in responding to the incoming
  stress: CRF shuts down the body's need for food
  and sex, and it increases alertness. Cortisol tells
  the body to produce more fuel for the muscles. In
  other words, the impulse for eating, sleeping, and
  reproductive activity is decreased, and alertness
  is increased. This makes good sense, for one must
  be prepared for danger.

What's the problem, then, if the fight or flight reaction
is an adaptive and helpful response? The problem occurs
when the body is repeatedly or chronically pushed into
this cycle. Maintenance of the flight or fight behaviors—a
decrease in appetite, sleep, sex, and an increase in agitation
and withdrawal are classic symptoms of depression. Researchers have found strong evidence that alterations in
the HPA cycle are present in depressed people. Here's
some of that evidence:

- Depressed people have higher levels of cortisol and CRF than normal people or people with other psychiatric disorders. This evidence has been found repeatedly since the 1960s, in numerous studies.

- Depressed people have more CRF-producing neurons in the hypothalamus than those who are not depressed.

- The CRF levels are decreased with antidepressants or electroconvulsant (electroshock) therapy.

At this point, there is strong evidence that the HPA axis plays an important role in the development or maintenance of depression. It may be that something we don't understand keeps the HPA cycle going. Or it might be stress (some people may be genetically susceptible to stress). Or it could be that repeated, early exposure to stress primes the HPA axis to be overactive and oversensitive.

Researchers at Emory University are studying the biological implications of childhood experiences on later adult life.[7] Exciting—but disturbing—new developments in biology are revealing indicators that adverse events early in life alter our bodies' biochemical functions, perhaps permanently. Here are some examples that give us clues to understand this body-mind mystery:

- Rat pups that are stressed in the early days of their lives—removed from their mothers for periods of time—showed changes in their HPA axis function that persisted well into their adult lives, long after the initial stress.[8]

- Newborn macaque monkeys who experience stressful conditions in early life grow up to exhibit behavioral and biochemical differences from adult macaque monkeys that were not stressed as newborns. Macaque mothers were placed in one of three different conditions: one where food was plentiful for her and her newborn, one where food was scarce, and one where the food level was unpredictable—sometimes plentiful and sometimes scarce. It was the mothers who were in the environment where food was unpredictable that had the greatest problems bonding with their newborns. In fact, they became so anxious and preoccupied about the food situation that they ignored their infants for long periods of time. It was these newborns that grew up to have the most problems. As adults, they shied away from new situations and avoided interactions with their peers. And, giving us a major clue about the mind-body connection, their HPA brain chemistries were different from their peers.[9]
- Rat pups exposed to stress (handling by human beings) developed different brain chemistry reactions. But the pups that received the most maternal care (licking and grooming) after the stress did the best; that is, their brain chemistry changed the least.[10]

The researchers spearheading many of these studies believe that the findings add up to an important theory: chronic repeated stress can produce lasting changes in the brain. These changes may lay the foundation for depression. Children who have been repeatedly exposed to abuse or neglect, for example, may have supersensitive fight or flight responses and, in adulthood, may develop depression in response to things that most people might be able to brush off.[11]

Biological Cycles

One of the most important rhythms of the body is its daily sleep schedule. Interruptions in this schedule may influence depression. While we might not go to sleep at the same time every night or wake up at the same time every morning, what happens while we are sleeping is intended to be finely tuned and regular. Every night, we drift in and out of five different sleep cycles. Any changes in the pattern of these cycles—whether we are conscious of them or not—can affect how we feel during the day. Researchers and sleep clinicians can observe sleep cycle patterns by hooking a person up to an electroencephalogram monitor (EEG). Researchers have found that when people are depressed, their sleep cycles are disrupted.[12] Typically, they spend less time in the stages of deep sleep and more time in REM, or dreamtime sleep. (REM stands for rapid eye movement; our eyes dart back and forth under our eyelids while we dream.) People who are depressed seem to enter REM sleep much faster than normal when they fall asleep.

It's commonly thought that depression causes sleep problems. But some theorists say the opposite may be true: a dysregulation of the sleep-wake cycle may be the root of the depressive disorder. It is true that sleep is critical to well-being, and any changes in it can have far-reaching effects. Some treatments for depression are based on this theory. The Japanese have developed *Morita therapy*, in which extensive sleep is prescribed for people who are extremely depressed.[13] Other methods of sleep therapy for depression recommend the opposite: decreasing the amount of sleep.

So far, we have looked at how the physical processes in the human body may cause depression or are affected by depression. But as the studies of identical twins have pointed out, something besides physiological processes contributes to depression. Environment—the circumstances in which people grow up and in which they live as adults—also influences depression.

Environmental Factors

Painful Childhoods

The events and experiences of childhood can contribute to depression. People with histories of either physical or sexual abuse in childhood are more likely to experience depression as adults.[14] Researchers also speculate, as the association is so strong, that biological changes in early childhood development may be responsible for the later depression. As we have seen from the previous discussion, ample evidence from research on the HPA axis supports this theory.

Painful childhoods do more, however, than simply alter our brain chemicals. Looking at child development from a psychosocial point of view, we see that children's understanding of themselves and their place in the world is something they learn. Psychoanalytic theory says that it is our earliest relationships—those with our mothers and fathers—that teach us how to think about the world, what to expect of others, how to feel about ourselves, and how to react to events. In other words, the beliefs we form when we are very young can influence all our future relationships.

For instance, at a very young age, we form our beliefs about whether or not we can trust others, and trust is the foundation upon which our future relationships are built. It is also in the earliest years that we form beliefs about whether or not we are worthwhile and lovable. We are all born utterly dependent. Growing up is a process of learning to be independent, to be separate from that all-important first caretaker and yet to form dependent, intimate relationships. Ideally, children learn during this long process that they can be separate individuals—be the people they really are inside—and be loved by someone else at the same time. If for some reason they learn the opposite—that their needs won't be met, that they can't be who they are and still be loved—they may decide that they don't deserve to be loved, that they are defective. When people don't know how to love themselves or how to form loving connections with others, the stage can be set for depression.

How does it happen that people form these negative beliefs about themselves and others? It can happen when children are neglected, ignored, or hurt. It can happen if a parent physically leaves a child through death or divorce, or emotionally through addiction, depression, or other disorders. But even people in the healthiest of relationships can be hurt and can develop negative beliefs. Nobody is to blame for this. While insensitive or cruel parents can and do hurt children both physically and emotionally, no parent is perfectly tuned in to a child's needs at all times, and some hurts are inevitable. No human being, on either side of the relationship—adult or child—can perfectly balance the needs for dependence and independence.

Regardless of what causes a difficulty, problems people have in their earliest relationships tend to recur later in life. The early beliefs people form about themselves and others can become lifelong patterns: the belief that others cannot be trusted, that others will always leave, and that they themselves are unlovable or defective. As people struggle to establish connections with others, these patterns and beliefs go before them and wreak havoc, leaving them vulnerable to isolation, loneliness, and low self-esteem—all ingredients for depression.

Physical, Sexual, and Emotional Abuse

The emotional impact of abuse is often severe and long lasting. The abuse may have been physical, sexual, or emotional; it may have been huge or seemingly small; it may have occurred during childhood or the adult years. But the memories of abuse are often painful. Some people try to deny the emotional impact, thinking the abuse was minor or that it occurred so long ago that it no longer matters. But denial does not lessen the pain. Many people who have experienced abuse are swept with feelings of despair, shame, and hopelessness even years after the abuse.

Some abuse survivors may have a pattern of feelings and experiences that fit another diagnostic category, called *post-traumatic stress disorder* (PTSD). Or they may experience both PTSD and major depression. Either way, the feelings that abuse survivors experience are real. But good therapy can help survivors begin to find their way out of the shadow of abuse.

Abuse is an especially important topic for many people who are recovering from addiction—the incidence of sexual abuse appears to be much higher in this group.[15] Uncovering memories of abuse can trigger a relapse. If you are recovering from addiction and have experienced abuse, it's important to get help for the feelings that abuse causes.

Related Factors Causing Depression

The world we live in produces pain, and as humans, we are affected both biologically and emotionally. For some people, pain in the form of trauma or loss leads to depression. Others have essentially learned how to be helpless in the face of everyday problems, which may lead them into depression. In the following sections, we'll take a look at the ways that trauma, loss, and helplessness are connected with depression.

Trauma

As we've seen in the preceding sections, childhood abuse and neglect may sow the seeds for later depression. As adults, we may think we are less vulnerable to the emotional impact of trauma, yet it still takes a heavy toll. Researchers in Israel followed up on emergency room patients who had experienced significant emotional trauma—car accidents, rapes, attacks, and other violence—and found that more than half (56 percent) of the people developed depression during the year after the traumatic event. And they found that people with a history of depression were more vulnerable to developing depression in response to these tragedies.[16] For example, if someone has struggled with depression in the past, being involved in a car accident where someone dies or witnessing a brutal event may trigger another episode of depression. People without a history of depression may still show all the signs of emotional trauma in response to a horrible event, but they are less likely to develop full-blown depression.

Losses

If people suffer extreme losses, they may develop depression. Any loss can produce grief and pain, but losing a loved one is one of the most painful things human beings have to bear. Being in relationships has been critical for survival and the continuation of the human species, but loss is inevitable and uncontrollable. People can do everything right, but others will still leave, whether by choice or by death. Other types of loss can also adversely affect people. Loss of anything that sustains them—a hobby, a pet, a job, or the ability to do certain activities as they grow older— can trigger a grief reaction. Over time, as people continue to suffer more loss—parents, family members, close friends, homes, jobs—the stage may be set for depression. Ultimately, loss can result in loneliness. Many people who are depressed feel very lonely, even if they have other people around them.

Why do some people who experience losses become depressed while others don't? As noted earlier in this chapter, some people are biologically more vulnerable to depression. Some people have had particularly difficult experiences with intimacy when they were young children, so they started on shaky ground. Others may have a solid foundation, but experience such painful or repeated losses that they cannot find their way out of grief. And because grief from the past accumulates, the loneliness they are feeling may be deeper than what might be reflected at the moment.

Learned Helplessness

As we grow up, ideally, we learn that we are competent individuals who are capable of taking on and succeeding at new tasks. We learn and believe that we are capable of giving and receiving love, and that we matter to other people. But some people learn just the opposite. They learn that no matter what they do, it is not good enough. Numerous experiences lead them to believe that they are deficient—that in spite of every effort, they will not succeed, obtain love, or gain a feeling of self-worth. They begin to feel helpless and hopeless. This, too, can set the stage for depression.

In studies, researchers have found that animals lose the will to live and grow if they are repeatedly hurt and can do nothing about it. For example, in one study, rats were placed in a pool designed so that no matter how hard they tried, they couldn't get out; the walls were too high and there were no dry places to climb up to. On other days, they were placed on a pad that delivered electric shocks, with nowhere to run away to. What happened to these rats? Over time, they stopped doing anything in these situations. In the pool, they didn't swim; they just floated, barely keeping their heads up out of the water. In the cage, they just stood on the electric pad without even trying to run away. This is called *learned helplessness*. It also might be called giving up. This is what happens to animals who are given no choices to alleviate their situation.[17]

It is sad to think about these animals in research experiments. It is tragic that this very same phenomenon occurs to human beings every day—not in scientific experiments, but in real life. It's not hard to understand how learned helplessness can happen to prisoners of war and victims of war-torn parts of the world. People in these situations have little control over what happens to them. But the same phenomenon can occur in relatively peaceful times in stable countries. Can you think of situations in which your behavior has no effect on what happens to you? Imagine yourself in a job where no matter what you do, your boss and co-workers are critical and negative. Or in a marriage where your spouse hits you even if you've prepared the perfect meal. Or in a family, as a child, where whatever you do to get noticed is met with disregard. Pretty soon, you might give up. This is learned helplessness.

If people are in a hurtful situation, and nothing they do will improve or change it, eventually they may begin to believe they are defective human beings. Unconsciously, they may begin judging *themselves* instead of the situation they are in. Instead of thinking, *This is an impossible relationship*, they begin telling themselves, *I am no good.* Even when new opportunities come along—the possibility of a new job, a new friend, a chance to begin again—it may be too late. Their helplessness has become hopelessness, and they don't try anymore. They remain stuck in their isolation and their feeling of worthlessness, both of which are ingredients of depression.

In these sections, we've looked at theories about how depression might be caused by biological makeup or environment. But indirect causes are possible too. Sometimes depression may be caused by, or made worse by, another issue.

Associated Factors

Sometimes depressive symptoms are part of another problem such as nicotine addiction or hormonal changes. In these situations, treating the main problem may help take care of the depression. Or simply understanding the relationship might help you tolerate the depression better while the main problem is being treated.

Hormonal Fluctuations

Hormones are intricately connected with neurotransmitters—the chemicals that carry messages between the nerve cells in the brain. Hormones are messengers, too, carrying information about the growth and development of all the body's systems. Changes in our hormonal levels can create changes in our brain's neurotransmitters—and consequently, our mood. In fact, we know that some hormonal diseases, like hypothyroidism, can cause depressive symptoms. *Hypothyroidism* occurs when the thyroid gland produces low levels of the thyroid hormone. Symptoms of hypothyroid disorder include fatigue, dry skin, and weight gain. Hypothyroidism is more common in women than men, and should be ruled out before a diagnosis of depression is made.

Many women can trace their mood swings to changes in their hormonal levels. Women's monthly menstrual cycles follow a delicate interchange among several hormones, but especially estrogen and progesterone. Anything that changes the balance in the hormones can influence depression. As a result, many women have special concerns about depression.

I'm on birth control pills.

Birth control pills can trigger or intensify depression in some women. For women who are prone to depression, this can be a special risk factor and a reason to consider another form of birth control.[18]

I just had a baby. I'm happy about it, but I don't feel the joy and excitement that I thought I would.

It is relatively normal to have the "baby blues" for about three to seven days after giving birth. But if this feeling continues, it may develop into what is known as *postpartum depression.*[19] This depression may be partly due to the stresses of having a newborn baby at home and all the responsibilities and changes that go along with it. But most likely, the changes in hormonal levels that occur during and after pregnancy alter the neurotransmitters and, as a result, mood.

If you have a history of depression, you may be at higher risk for postpartum depression. Some women are ashamed to be depressed after they've had a baby, because they believe they should be happy. They're reluctant to tell people how they really feel. Postpartum depression is real, and it happens to about 13 percent of new mothers across a wide range of cultures.[20] Being depressed does not mean you are an unworthy parent! But it does mean that you need—and deserve—to get help as soon as possible so that you and your baby can get started on a healthy track. And women aren't the only ones to experience an increase in depression around the time a baby is born. Men, especially those in stepfamilies and those who are partners of unmarried mothers, may be prone to depression during this time too.[21]

My depression is worse during the days before my period.

We've all heard jokes about PMS (premenstrual syndrome), so it's easy to come to the conclusion that PMS isn't a very serious problem. But some women are severely affected by the physical and emotional changes that occur during the week before menses.

PMS has been also called *premenstrual dysphoric disorder* and is recognized as an actual emotional disorder, not just something that a woman is imagining.[22] The criteria for premenstrual dysphoric disorder are similar to the symptoms of depression:

- Feelings of depression, hopelessness, or low self-worth
- Anxiety, tension, and edginess
- Tearfulness and oversensitivity to criticism or rejection

- Irritability and anger
- Decreased interest in things that usually give joy or pleasure
- Difficulty concentrating
- Fatigue, sleeping a great deal
- Overeating and craving certain foods (especially starches)
- Feeling overwhelmed or out of control
- Physical symptoms such as bloating, breast tenderness, joint pain, headaches, or weight gain

Women who have a history of depression may be especially vulnerable to premenstrual dysphoric disorder. For example, Zoe was very aware of her vulnerability:

My depression is majorly affected by my PMS. I am quite stable until a week before my menstrual cycle, and then severe depression sets in. I am pretty much suicidal.

Lara noticed a similar pattern:

The week I'm expecting my period I start getting down on myself a lot.

Some women are not attuned to their bodies and may not recognize the relationship between their mood states and natural cycles. This is unfortunate, because there is a solution for most of these situations. A gynecologist can do a thorough assessment and suggest ideas that may involve regulating a woman's hormone system. Time and patience are needed in making the adjustment, but it can greatly improve a person's life.

Other women are relieved just to know the pattern exists. They can tolerate the feelings of depression because they know their source and they know the feelings will pass in a few days. For instance, LaVonda struggled with depression through most of her life. She recognized that she had a particularly difficult time during the days before her period, but she learned to identify those times and ride them out. For many women, just knowing where they are in their menstrual phase can offer great reassurance; what they're reacting to may very well be real, but the intensity of their response may be magnified by the shift in hormones.

I'm middle-aged but not in menopause yet, and my moods are really changing.

Symptoms of depression can be related to hormonal changes in midlife. Years before menstrual periods actually stop, subtle symptoms may appear. This phase is called the *perimenopausal phase,* or "around the menopause." Many women may be prepared for mood swings with actual menopause, but most are not even thinking about the changes in hormonal levels that begin years before this. As a result, the mood swings of perimenopause surprise them. Some of the same symptoms that occur during PMS can occur during perimenopause.

I'm in menopause and I know my depression is at least partly related to that.

Not all women experience depression during menopause. But for some, depressive symptoms can be severe. A woman who is concerned about depression during menopause may want to consider estrogen replacement therapy. Estrogen is often recommended during menopause to protect women against bone loss and heart disease. There are pros and cons to using estrogen replacement; one benefit is that it may decrease the depression associated with menopause. The best course of action is to see a gynecologist familiar with a wide range of options for treating depression during menopause.

Nicotine

Many people who are depressed find it much harder to quit smoking than people who are not depressed.[23] Smokers may not even recognize that they are depressed because nicotine acts as a stimulant or upper. In this way, smoking can be a form of self-medication. The nicotine may produce two effects: (1) it may change low mood by affecting the brain's neurotransmitters, and (2) it can act as a stimulant, giving an energy boost. As long as people continue to smoke, they can hold many depressed feelings at bay. Whether smokers have major depression or more subtle feelings such as sadness, hopelessness, or anxiety, they may not recognize that they are depressed. Then, of course, they cannot recognize that their depression is making it hard for them to stop smoking.

When people who are depressed try to quit smoking, they may feel a tremendous amount of emotional pain and sadness. This is more than a sense of grief about not having cigarettes. It is more than the irritability and craving that most smokers feel during withdrawal. For some, it is the reemergence of depression that has been mostly hidden or at least controlled. The depression may be so intense that they decide they would rather smoke—with all its dangers and consequences—than experience the depression. Because women have a higher rate of depression, they are especially prone to being depressed cigarette smokers.

Cara experienced this kind of problem. She was forty-five years old, successful at work, in a loving relationship, and was the type of person people enjoyed being around.

> *I've always been a real joker and liked to make people laugh. That's how others see me. But when I try to quit smoking, it's a whole new ball game. I hate to even try quitting when I'm working full time because I know I'll just sit at my desk and cry. I don't know what happens to me. Everyone else is amazed too. And worried. I know I need to quit smoking, but I'm scared to even try. I get so depressed, I can barely work.*

Does this mean that cigarette smokers who are depressed are simply doomed to continued smoking? Not at all. Research suggests that people can cope if they get vigorous therapy for depression during the withdrawal period. Some very promising research has been done using cognitive-behavioral therapy—a therapy that teaches people strategies to endure and lessen negative mood states—for smokers who are depressed and trying to quit smoking. Surprisingly, there is no research on the use of antidepressants for people who are depressed and are trying to quit smoking.

In one study, conducted at the Department of

Psychiatry at the University of California in San Francisco, smokers who were depressed were given two forms of treatment. One group received cognitive-behavioral therapy and the other received simple encouragement and support. Six months after treatment, half of the smokers who had received cognitive-behavioral treatment were still not smoking. In comparison, only 12 percent of the group who had just received support and encouragement were not smoking. The researchers speculate that the cognitive-behavioral treatment might have helped the smokers deal with both their depression and their nicotine withdrawal symptoms.[24]

There is growing acceptance in the United States that the pleasures of smoking are not worth the health risks. As a result, many people have quit smoking and using tobacco products.

More people are also becoming aware that cigarette smoking may be a sign of depression. An article in the *Journal of Family Practice*, for example, recommends that physicians (a) view smoking as a sign that a patient may have an underlying depressive disorder and (b) assess and treat the depression.[25] Now that the link between cancer, other serious health problems, and nicotine is understood, it's clear that using nicotine to control depression is not a good option.

If you are a smoker who's having trouble quitting, you might have an underlying depression. If so, it's especially important for you to get help with that illness. Both psychotherapy and antidepressants may be useful. But whatever kinds of help you choose, it's important that you know you may experience at least some symptoms of depression while you are going through nicotine withdrawal. These symptoms may include crying or having feelings of hopelessness. But this doesn't mean you are spiraling into a full depression. As you learn ways to cope with your depression, you'll be able to maintain your new nicotine-free life.

Alcoholic Homes

Children of alcoholics are not automatically depressed. In fact, most research studies find that the majority of children of alcoholics do not experience major depression or any other disorders.[26] But if you are involved in a self-help group such as Adult Children of Alcoholics (ACA), you may object. You may think, *I see how alcoholism or addiction has affected children! Every week in my group, many people talk about their depression, and many are in therapy or on antidepressants. How can you say that being an adult child of an alcoholic and being depressed are not related?* When you attend groups such as ACA, you may see many adult children of alcoholics who are depressed, because going to these groups is one of the ways they are seeking help for their depression. Therefore, their numbers may be over-represented in Adult Children of Alcoholics groups.

Possible Environmental Contributions to Depression in Alcoholic Homes

Still, there is no doubt that in some alcoholic families, the environment can be ripe for developing depression. First, the alcoholic parent and the child may not be able to bond with each other because the alcohol or other drug use is in the way. If the parents are continually impaired, they may not be able to pay attention to the child in the careful and consistent way that promotes bonding.

Second, the child may be forced to trade roles with the adult, disrupting the process of gaining independence. The child may end up taking care of the alcoholic's needs. For instance, the child makes supper or gets younger siblings off to school because Mom or Dad is too impaired. Sometimes taking care of parents' needs is more subtle. It can mean that the child is working far too hard to excel at school or sports so that Mom or Dad won't be disappointed and get drunk. These are not supportive, happy situations for a child.

Third, there may be abuse in alcoholic homes. The family may be split apart. The growing children can feel despair at having no impact on what is happening around them. Or, perhaps worse, they may mistakenly believe that they are the cause of all the turmoil. Children who absorb these beliefs about themselves will struggle in future relationships and may be prone to depression.

Possible Biological Contributions to Depression in Alcoholic Homes

In some cases, biology contributes to depression in children of addicts. The children may inherit a genetic predisposition toward depression. In some families, alcoholism, anxiety, and depression seem to occur together. Sylvia notes:

> On my mother's side of the family there's a lot of depression and alcoholism. My mother was depressed

*and so were her sisters and her mother. My two broth-
ers and my dad were alcoholic. My dad was also depressed—in fact, he killed himself.*

This type of pattern has led theorists to speculate
whether there is something called the *depression spectrum
disease.* They hypothesize that whatever is being genetically transmitted shows up mostly as depression in women
and as alcoholism in men. The National Institute of Mental
Health funded a large study of depression to test this theory. They found that alcoholic women often had both depression and alcoholism in their families. They also found
that the alcoholism, particularly among the women family
members, was often a by-product of a primary depression.
But this wasn't so for alcoholic men; their alcoholism
seemed to run more true—their relatives are more likely to
be alcoholic than depressed.[27]

But several genetic studies since then have found little
connection between depression and addiction in generations of families, and there is no definitive research on the
subject. It might be that the environmental or emotional
factors are so big they overshadow biological factors. In
other words, the stress and trauma of living with an alcoholic parent, and the emotional toll that takes, may play a
bigger role in developing depression than a particular genetic makeup. Still, the question remains, *Is there a genetic
link between depression and addiction, and if so, what is it?* It
may be that some people inherit a special sensitivity to alcohol or drugs. It may also be that they inherit a deficiency
in serotonin, one of the natural chemicals in the brain,
which seems to play an important role in depression.

Another possibility is that some people inherit serotonin levels that change significantly in the presence of alcohol. It may also be that there are two types of connections between depression and addiction: genetic and environmental. For some people, the connection may be largely genetic. Their family histories are filled with examples of both depression and alcoholism, and indeed, some people have both disorders. In other families, there is very little overlap between depression and alcoholism.

Eating Disorders

Depression often develops along with eating disorders, particularly bulimia. People with bulimia go on eating binges; some may vomit or take laxatives afterward. For most people, the eating disorder occurs first, and the depression follows. Shame, low self-worth, and feelings of hopelessness often develop as the eating disorder takes hold. These feelings are part of depression too.

Medications for Blood Pressure and Other Physical Problems

Medications for various physical disorders can cause or contribute to depression. When depression is inadvertently caused by medication, it is called *iatrogenic depression*. For example, interferon, used in the treatment of hepatitis C, AIDS, and some cancers, causes depression in 25 to 40 percent of patients who take it.[28] If you are on any kind of medication, consult with your physician about possible side effects that may be producing depression. But never just stop taking your medications! Medications change the body's chemical balance, and changing it suddenly may be dangerous. Physicians usually can find other medications that can treat the physical problem without causing depression, or they can make other recommendations.

Sometimes older people who are on multiple medications experience depression. Family members, friends, and sometimes even doctors may assume it's just a normal grief reaction that comes with age and loss. But in some cases the medications themselves—or the interactions among them—may actually be the culprit. Again, talking to a physician is very important.

Traumatic Brain Injury

Depression can occur after brain injury. Brain injury commonly occurs after severe automobile accidents, falls, or other accidents causing head trauma. The immediate symptoms, such as memory or thinking problems, are the ones that people are most concerned about. After time and rehabilitation, depression and anxiety may appear. Some people are surprised and confused about this, thinking, *I survived; why am I depressed?* They may not know that depression is common after head injury, and needs as much attention as the more obvious aftereffects. In fact, depression occurs in 26 to 60 percent of people recovering from major head injury.[29]

Seasonal Changes

Seasonal affective disorder (SAD) occurs primarily in northern latitudes during the winter months, when the days are shorter.[30] Therefore, the strongest theory about SAD is that it is caused by a lack of light. We need a certain amount of light each day to regulate our hormones, especially one called *melatonin*. Since hormones are intricately connected with the balance of neurotransmitters in the brain, a change in these critical hormones can produce unwanted changes in the level of neurotransmitters.

Serotonin, too, may play a role in seasonal affective disorder. Some research suggests that serotonin levels naturally fall during the winter months and that some foods, such as carbohydrates, increase serotonin levels. These ideas fit in quite well with symptoms of SAD: people with SAD usually feel worse in the winter and crave carbohydrates.

Alcohol and Other Drugs

The chemicals we put in our bodies affect our natural chemical balance, which is designed to keep our moods stable. Here's an overview of the effects of various substances on our moods and states of mind.[31]

Alcohol

Alcohol is a depressant. It slows or depresses the body's general level of activity.

Sleeping Pills and Anxiety-Reducers

Barbiturates and tranquilizers, such as Xanax, Halcion, and Ativan are also depressants. A person taking them may feel sedated. For people who are already depressed or who have a tendency toward depression, these types of drugs may bring the depression—and possibly suicidal thinking—to the surface.

Marijuana

Long-term marijuana use can cause *amotivational syndrome*. In this state, people don't care about participating in life or doing much of anything. The effects of long-term marijuana use can resemble depression.[32]

Opiates

Opiates are painkillers. Withdrawal from opiates can include feelings of anxiety, fear, and dread. Even normal life events can seem extraordinarily painful if you are used to medicating pain and then stop doing so.

Cocaine and Other Stimulants

Three to five days after use, a cocaine user may experience a "crash", or period of sadness. This is part of the withdrawal process. For some people, it may linger on, complicating diagnosis.[33] This is thought to be a rebound effect—the depressed mood is a reaction to the euphoria that the use of cocaine or other stimulants creates.

Gender

While the basic causes of depression may be the same for everyone, women may be more vulnerable to depression than men. The rate of depression among women is about twice as high as it is for men.[34] Clinicians often note that relationships are especially important to women, and they may be more prone to depression when relationships are disrupted.[35] Women may also be more apt to evaluate themselves negatively, resulting in low self-esteem. In society, women often face more responsibility for families, more financial difficulties, discrimination, loss of opportunity, and domestic violence, all of which can contribute to depression.

What If I Am Recovering from Addiction?

Using Chemicals

People in addiction recovery often have used chemicals that can create or magnify depressive symptoms. It isn't known whether the effects are short term or long lasting. Some theorists believe that long-term exposure to drugs creates changes in the brain that may take weeks, months, or even years to reverse. This, of course, is particularly true for people who have used a lot of drugs for a long time. Some of these changes in the brain may leave a person an addict. In other words, the body remembers the disease, and the disease begins again if drug use is resumed. But it is also possible that the changes produced alter the body's response to pleasure and reward. These changes may leave people more vulnerable to depression—and even more so if they were already vulnerable to depression for some other reason.

Using Nicotine

Alcoholics and other addicts have much higher rates of smoking than the general population. This is one of the great ironies for people in addiction recovery. They avoid the tragedy of dying from alcohol or other drug use, only to die of nicotine use. Some alcoholics and addicts do not want to quit smoking because they are afraid the stress of quitting might trigger a relapse to their alcohol or other drug use. However, research doesn't bear out this fear. A research study looking at people who quit alcohol or other drugs and nicotine at the same time found that their relapse rates to alcohol or drugs were about the same as for people who kept smoking.[36] In other words, quitting smoking did not set them up for relapse.

If you are in addiction recovery and are depressed, you may be especially afraid to quit smoking. As you read earlier in this chapter, nicotine can hold depressed feelings at bay. However, you can get help for depression. Then, when you have a more stable emotional foundation, you'll be able to stop using tobacco. As a bonus, your self-esteem— knowing you've beaten the nicotine addiction—will probably be higher.

What Does This Mean for Me?

It you are depressed, it may be hard to put your finger on the exact cause. Depression is a complicated phenomenon, and people are such delicate, finely tuned animals that the exact cause of depression may never be known. But you can be assured that rarely do people bring it on themselves.

For most people, there won't be one simple cause; usually several events must conspire to create this painful disorder. To complicate matters further, a factor that causes depression in one case may actually be a result of depression in another. For example, an imbalance of neurotransmitters may cause a person to become isolated, which in turn can lead to depression. In this case, the chemical imbalance in the brain would be the cause of depression and the isolation would be the result. On the other hand, forced helplessness or isolation can cause changes in brain chemistry. In this case, the apparent imbalance in brain chemistry would be the result of the isolation rather than the cause.

Exploring the possible causes of depression can give some sense of control to a person who feels helpless and overwhelmed. But whether or not people understand the causes of their depression, treatment can usually help them cope with, or recover from, depression.

Further Questions

I struggle with depression. People say that depression is hereditary; does this mean my children will become depressed too?

No, not necessarily. Even though there does seem to be a genetic role in the development of depression—especially bipolar disorder—most children of depressed people do not become depressed. Creating a healthy environment to grow up in can help decrease any child's chances of growing up with depression. However, we do not yet know what part of depression is due to genetics and what part is due to the world and events around us. Therefore, we cannot predict who will become depressed.

My parents were alcoholics when I grew up, and now I am an adult experiencing depression. Is being depressed part of being an adult child of an alcoholic?

Being an adult child of an alcoholic can mean many things. Some parents do not develop alcoholism until late in life, so its impact on their children may be relatively small. Or, the parent who is not addicted may be able to take over the family in a way that minimizes the effect of the other parent's illness. Or, biologically, the genetic load for addiction and other problems is not transmitted. In other words, there is no automatic relationship between being a child of an alcoholic and being depressed. In fact, most research studies find that the majority of children of alcoholics do not experience major depression or any other psychiatric disorders.[37]

Isn't depression simply a chemical imbalance?

Our best understanding is that depressed people do have alterations in important brain chemicals. Because the brain is so mysterious and unavailable to study, the chemical reactions in it cannot actually be seen or measured. But chemical imbalance is a good theory for several reasons: (1) It fits with what is known about treatment of depression. For example, antidepressants seem to work by changing the levels of important brain chemicals. (2) It leads to good ideas about more biochemical treatment methods to explore. (3) It helps take away the stigma that so many people feel about being depressed. The chemical imbalance theory has one important shortcoming: it only tells us what is happening at a moment in time; it doesn't tell us what causes what. As we have seen in this chapter, we now know that environmental stress, in childhood or adulthood, can cause changes in a person's brain chemistry. And, no doubt, it can happen the other way around too: changes in brain chemistry—which may occur for reasons we don't know—can produce depression.

Some people who explain their depression as a chemical imbalance only take antidepressants and yet see improvements; they do not work on their own or with a therapist to understand the nature of their depression and what they can change in their lives to improve it. Although this works for some people, most people with depression need more than a strictly biological approach to treatment.

What Can I Do to Help Myself?

It may seem as if depression comes from nowhere, for no reason. But this isn't true; depression comes from somewhere, even if you can't easily identify the reason. Once you begin to understand what may cause or at least worsen your depression, you may see ways to overcome, lessen, or prevent it.

1. This chapter has described many possible causes of depression. Review the factors listed on pages 83–86. Do you think any of these may have caused your depression? Put a check mark (✓) next to the items that apply to you.

- *There is a history of depression in my family.* Think back to your parents and their brothers and sisters. Has anyone had depression? What about your grandparents? Are there any patterns of depression going back several generations? When you look for such patterns, you may not find depression per se. Depression was not always officially diagnosed in earlier generations because so little was known about it then. To discover whether there is a history of depression in your family, you may have to think about how these people would be viewed nowadays. If you are adopted, do you know anything about the mental health of your biological relatives?

- *I had a particularly painful childhood.* How stable was your home life growing up? Did you form a warm and welcoming bond with at least one parent? Did the adults in your life meet your physical and emotional needs? If you aren't sure what your childhood was like, you might be able to find out from other relatives.

- *I have experienced significant losses in my life.* Think back to important people or things that you no longer have in your life. These might include friends and family members, pets, and even activities or abilities. When did these losses occur? Did you have the time and support to cope with them?

- *I use negative self-talk.* Spend a day noticing how you talk to yourself. What thoughts do you have in your own mind about who you really are? Are you positive and accepting, or do you constantly put yourself down? Are there any words you automatically use to talk to yourself when you are in difficult situations? Do you blame yourself or do you coach yourself along?

- *I have experienced physical, sexual, or emotional abuse.* If you have experienced abuse, have you gotten help for it? Or have you tried to put it out of your mind and assume it has no relevance to your life now? For many people, the effects of abuse stay with them for many years.

- *I am struggling with an eating disorder.* If you have an eating disorder, have you sought help? If you are attending a self-help group or seeing a therapist, have you talked about the possibility of depression?

- *I am taking medication for high blood pressure or another physical disorder.* If you are taking any medication, could you talk to your physician about the possibility of depression being a side effect?

- *My natural hormonal cycles are affecting me.* If you are a woman, are you aware of your natural hormonal cycles and how they may be affecting you?

— Do you experience premenstrual symptoms? Some women rate their mood every day on their calendar, using a scale from one to ten, with one being totally downhearted and ten being ecstatic. Over a period of three to six months, you should be able to discern a pattern, if there is one.

— Have you recently had a baby?

— Are you in your early to mid-forties, or expecting to reach menopause within the next three to five years? If so, you may be in the perimenopause phase and could therefore begin experiencing depressive symptoms.

— Have you reached menopause? If so, and if you are experiencing depressive symptoms, have you discussed options with your physician?

- *I have noticed that I experience increased depression during certain seasons.* Do you sleep more, feel more tired, eat more during the winter or the summer months? Some people become depressed, or find their depression worsens, in certain seasons of the year. Most often, seasonal affective disorder occurs in the winter months, but it can also occur in the summer.

- *I am taking sleeping pills or tranquilizers.* Some of their side effects include depression.

- *I am in early recovery from alcohol or drug addiction.* Some of the residual effects of drugs can cause depressive symptoms.

2. Look back over the list of possible causes of depression. Notice which ones you checked. Knowing what may be contributing to your depression can give you hope and may guide you in the steps you need to take to get better. Just as there are often reasons for depression, there are solutions. As you reflect on these thoughts, is there anyone you can talk to?

Chapter 4

Depression and Death

Death . . . was a daily presence, blowing over me in cold gusts.

~ William Styron, about his depression

While most people understand that depression greatly decreases the quality of life, not everyone knows that depression can threaten life itself. Depression has two lethal connections: suicide and greater mortality due to other diseases. We'll take a look at each of them here.

The Lethal Connections of Depression

Depression and Suicide

Worldwide, suicide causes more deaths than war. According to the Centers for Disease Control, more than 30,000 people in the United States kill themselves each year. Though the suicide rates in the United States have been gradually decreasing overall, some segments of the population are particularly vulnerable: from 1980 to 1997, the rate of suicide among young people from ages fifteen through nineteen has increased by 11 percent, and the rate among children from ages ten through fourteen has doubled.[1] Suicide among black children and teenagers has been increasing at even greater rates.[2] According to the Centers for Disease Control, of all the age groups, the risk of suicide is highest among the elderly, with more than six thousand people over the age of fifty-five killing themselves each year. Suicide "epidemics" can occur, generally in distinct geographical locations, where several suicides occur over time. This sometimes happens with young people, where it may be that death becomes glorified, or the person who initially commits suicide is revered.

While every suicidal person is different, common factors propelling a person toward suicide include hopelessness, shame, and what is perceived as intolerable psychological pain.[3]

What Can You Do If Someone You Know Is Suicidal?

If someone you know is struggling with depression, there may be some warning signs that indicate the person is thinking of suicide. They may include

- displaying an unexpected upswing in mood and/or saying things like, "I can see an end to my problems"
- making final arrangements, giving things away, making sure his or her will and insurance is up-to-date, getting papers and other belongings in order
- showing feelings of extreme hopelessness, humiliation, or shame

- being upset over a recent breakup of an important relationship
- talking of "things being better if I were dead"
- risk-taking, having a lack of concern about his or her own welfare

If you notice any of these signs, or wonder if your friend is considering suicide, the best thing to do is to talk to him or her. It's a common fallacy that bringing up the subject will somehow drive people closer to killing themselves. Chances are, they have already thought about it to some degree and may be relieved to have the chance to talk about it. Or they may be grateful that you are concerned. If you find that the person is thinking about suicide or has a plan "just in case," it's time to take action. Call a mental health emergency number in your area or go to an emergency clinic. You may wonder if you are overreacting, but that's far better than regretting an action you didn't take.

While most suicides can be prevented, you need to know that doing all the right things may not stop a person from killing himself or herself. While this can create a feeling of helplessness, letting go of the idea that you can or should be able to control the outcome of someone's life frees you—and, one hopes, them—to choose life and to live it fully.

What Can You Do If You Are Suicidal?

1. *Tell someone.* The most important thing you can do is to not keep your feeling a secret. You may feel like your situation is hopeless or that no one

has any better answers than you do. Your despair, humiliation, anger, or other emotions cloud rational thinking. You may be embarrassed or ashamed of your thoughts. You might be intensely ambivalent, wanting to die on the one hand, but wanting a reason to live. By taking some time out and talking to someone else, you are giving yourself a chance to reconsider and learn what your options are. And there *are* options, beyond what you may know at this moment. Call a local hot line or go to an emergency clinic. Ask a friend or family member to go with you.

2. *Don't "practice" suicide.* Rehearsing a plan in your mind, going to a site where you might kill yourself, or making attempts that you know will fail may lower your threshold for another, more lethal attempt later on. If you find yourself doing this, seek help right away. Tell your therapist if you have one, or find a professional you can talk to.

3. *Make a contract.* Write a promise with someone else—a therapist or another professional you can trust—that you will not act on suicidal thoughts. Write down what you will do instead—for example, make a phone call, write in a journal, or go where there are people.

4. *Make a safety plan.* Living with yourself when you are suicidal is analogous to living with a vio-

lent partner. Women who live with violent men are often advised to make a plan to keep themselves safe the next time their spouse becomes violent. This is also the care you need to take to protect yourself against your own violence. If you struggle with recurring thoughts of suicide, take a step back and think about what you need to do to keep yourself safe. Your plan might include removing a gun or other weapon from the premises; not having a large quantity of medications on hand; not living alone; not walking across high bridges; not reading books, stories, or poems (or listening to music) about death and suicide. You will know your own danger zones and can make a personal commitment to keep yourself out of danger.

5. *Don't drink or use drugs.* If you are suicidal, mood-altering chemicals—even in small quantities—may make you act on impulses that you normally wouldn't have otherwise.

While in the midst of depression, suicide can seem like the only option. But with treatment and the passage of time, the idea of suicide as a solution fades. William Styron wrote a book about his depression to give hope to others: "It is of great importance that those who are suffering a siege perhaps for the first time, be told—be convinced rather—that the illness will run its course and that they will pull through."[4]

Depression and "Natural" Death

Most depressed people do not choose suicide. However, surprisingly, depression itself seems to shorten the normal life span and to cause what some have called *accelerated physical aging*. A Harvard researcher, Dr. George Valliant, has spent much of his life doing a longitudinal study on inner-city men. He has found a strong correlation between depression, illness, and death. From his study of this large group of men over most of their lifetimes, he concludes that the "risk of affective disorders may lie along a continuum. At one extreme may be men with stable lifestyles, a lifelong resistance to mood disorder, and unusually good physical health late in life. At the other extreme of the continuum may be men with vulnerability to mood disorder and disease."[5]

Some of the factors making a depressed person more vulnerable to disease and death are fairly obvious: depressed people are more likely to smoke, are not as physically active, have poor eating habits, and have more alcohol problems. But even after taking these into consideration, the differences in mortality are evident in study after study:

- A longitudinal aging study in Amsterdam followed more than three thousand people between the ages of fifty-five and eighty-five for five years. They found that people who were depressed were almost twice as likely to die during that time period, primarily from heart disease.[6]

- The Centers for Disease Control keeps databases on large groups of people, one of which is called the National Health and Nutrition Epidemiological Study data. Researchers examined this group of 2,832 individuals over the age of forty-five who were free of disease and had normal lab values for 12.5 years. Controlling for all known heart risk factors (smoking, weight, activity, blood pressure, and cholesterol), they found that people who had high levels of depression were more likely to develop and to die of heart disease.[7]

- Researchers at Columbia University reviewed all the studies examining the relationship between depression and death. Looking at the most recent studies, they found that five out of six found a relationship between depression and cardiovascular disease. The risk of developing heart disease was one and one-half to four times higher for depressed people, compared with those who were not depressed. These researchers concluded that "it is now abundantly clear that depression is associated with ischemic heart disease." Further, they found that patients with heart disease or who have had heart attacks have worse outcomes if they are depressed, with mortality rates three to four times higher than nondepressed people.[8]

- Researchers at the Mayo Clinic followed up on 523 patients who had taken psychological tests thirty years earlier that could categorize them as either optimists or pessimists. They found that those people categorized as optimists had better survival rates than expected, and pessimists had a 19 percent higher death rate.[9]

Why does depression make a person more vulnerable to disease and death? One clue is the effect of sudden distress. We know that rates of heart attacks are considerably higher during times of catastrophe. For example, on the day of the major Northridge earthquake in Los Angeles, there was a considerable rise in the number of cardiac arrests.[10]

It may be that some of the same factors are involved in long-term distress. As discussed in chapter 3—the section on the HPA axis on page 51—one new and promising theory of depression is that it is caused by the body continuously being in a "flight or fight" mode, producing an overabundance of cortisol. It is possible that this high level of cortisol causes not only depression, but heart disease as well.[11] A related factor may be that there appears to be increased blood platelet aggregation (arteriosclerosis) associated with depression.[12]

What If I Am Recovering from Addiction?

It's especially important for you to avoid relapse to any alcohol or drug use. Any use is likely to lead to uncontrolled use, which in turn leaves you more vulnerable to self-destructive impulses.

Now is the time to pay special attention to how well you are taking care of your body. Your alcoholism or addiction may have already taken a toll on your health, so now during depression, your body needs all the help it can get.

What Does This Mean for Me?

When you're depressed, you're more vulnerable to getting sick. What (even small) things can you do to take care of your health?

Further Question

I'm not sure I want to live anyway.

It's hard to choose life when you are being pulled in the opposite direction by depression. The most important thing you can do is to allow time to take its course, as time will lead you away from depression. And, while you are waiting for time—and therapy or medications—to help, make choices that will keep yourself healthy and whole for when you are well again.

What Can I Do to Help Myself?

1. Review the list on pages 89–91. Which of those things can you do to keep yourself safe? Are you willing to do them? Who can you ask to help you?

2. If you are suicidal, imagine yourself in another time and place, where you have choices and possibilities. If anything were possible in your life right now, what would you choose? Let yourself sit in a quiet place with this question for at least

ten minutes. When you are finished, write or draw what you imagined. Now ask yourself what would make your dream possible. Is there even a small way you could start? People who feel suicidal often feel like they are trapped, with no hope. But often, the boundaries they've set or imagined are artificial and self-created. For example, you might imagine, *I'd love to travel around the world . . . but that's not possible because I have to work.* Or, *I've always wanted to be a professional photographer, but that's really unrealistic.* In both these cases, the ideas *are* possible and realistic. You can change your entire career and work for low wages doing what you love; you could take language or photography classes that will prepare you for your dream. In either case, the choices—even if they shake up your life entirely—will have far fewer ramifications than ending your life altogether. Finding a therapist who will help you explore the boundaries you've set on your life, and break free of them, might be a place to start.

Chapter 5

What Can I Do about My Depression? Psychotherapy

Tell me, what is it you plan to do with your one wild and precious life?

~ Mary Oliver

Telling a person with depression to just cheer up is like telling a drug addict to just say no to drugs. Once a person becomes depressed, willpower has little or no effect. Depression is an illness that runs its own course. However, effective treatment is more available now than ever before. And most people who recover from depression are amazed at how much better their lives become after treatment.

The two main treatments for depression are medication and psychotherapy, or a combination of both. Different people respond to different types of treatment. A psychologist, social worker, or psychiatrist can do a thorough assessment and recommend the best type of treatment for a particular individual. Some people start with psychotherapy and later add medication; others start with both psychotherapy and medication. This chapter looks at psychotherapy, and chapter 7 looks at medications. Either way, it's also critical to pay attention to lifestyle factors, which are covered in chapter 6.

What Is Psychotherapy?

Psychotherapy is talk therapy. *What good will it do to talk about my depression?* you may wonder. But psychotherapy is more than just talking about depression; it is a way to help people understand their depression—its causes, its effects, and its management. Psychotherapy can be extremely effective and often is the treatment of choice for depression. It can help break the cycle of depression. The therapist can be a companion in the darkness, helping people to see where they are and to find a way out.

The psychotherapy component of treatment is important for three reasons. First, uncovering the sources of depression can give people ideas and courage to try new ways of living. Making these changes may decrease or eliminate the depression. Second, people can learn where their vulnerabilities lie, so that they may be able to anticipate and prevent future depressive episodes. Third, it's a great relief for people to get some support and understanding from an objective person.

There are many approaches to psychotherapy, many more than we can examine in this book. We will discuss generally how psychotherapy works. Then we will take a closer look at cognitive-behavioral therapy, an approach that was designed specifically for the treatment of depression.[1]

Most of the various approaches to therapy cover some common ground. Here are some of the main topics that are typically discussed in therapy. How deeply any of these are explored depends on you and your therapist's approach.

- *Assessment.* At the beginning of therapy, your therapist will probably ask many specific questions to discover whether you are suffering from depression. (Many of these questions will be similar to those you asked yourself in chapter 1.) As therapy goes on, your therapist will continue to evaluate the severity and persistence of your symptoms of depression and make recommendations accordingly.

- *Childhood.* How happy were you as a child? Is there depression in your family? When you were growing up, how did you learn to deal with your feelings? Were there any traumatic events in your childhood that could be affecting how you feel about yourself and your world today?

- *Current and past relationships.* How much support have you had in your life? Are you able to establish intimate relationships? Are you lonely?

- *Unresolved grief.* What loss have you experienced in your life? Have you had the time and safety you've needed to resolve this grief? Is grief affecting you today?

- *Stress.* What everyday stressors are you experiencing in your life now? Can any of them be lessened?

Over the course of several sessions, you and your therapist will begin to see patterns in the ways you think, feel, and act in the world. Many of these patterns are healthy and sustaining, but others are self-defeating and keep depression going.

One reason people often (and inadvertently) continue negative patterns is because there is something they still need to learn. For example, people who repeatedly select friends who are unkind may continue to do so until they realize they have a right to compassion and respect. When they can see this and believe it, they will begin to choose new friends. However, if they don't see the pattern and their part in it, they are likely to repeat it.

People also continue negative patterns of living because the behavior served them well at one time. For example, those who learned as small children not to challenge authority because they got severely punished may continue to be passive as adults, even in the most demeaning situations. When we're children, being passive may mean survival. When we're adults, it can mean not getting important needs met. It's very difficult to immediately drop old behaviors when they become ineffective. But therapy gives people another perspective and the support needed to make changes.

Cognitive-Behavioral Therapy and the Circle of Change

Cognitive-behavioral therapy, which was designed specifically to treat depression, has undergone extensive research and refinement. In fact, some research has now shown treatment with antidepressants and treatment with cognitive-behavioral therapy to be equally effective. A major study published in the *American Journal of Psychiatry*, by researchers at the University of Pennsylvania, compared the outcomes of antidepressants and psychotherapy. To do this, they analyzed the data from four independent studies and found that even for severe depression, there was no difference in the recovery from depression between those who received antidepressants and those who received cognitive-behavioral therapy.[2] Even for people taking medications, cognitive-behavioral therapy can help, and many therapists today incorporate aspects of it into their work. For example, several studies have been done to look at *residuals* of depression after treatment with medication. Residuals are low-level symptoms of depression (e.g., irritability, anxiety, low mood) that may remain after the full-blown episode of depression has waned. Patients who received cognitive-behavioral therapy in addition to their medication had far fewer relapses over an eighteen-month period than people who received medication alone.[3]

The therapist using cognitive-behavioral therapy helps people examine their thinking and try new ways of acting in the world. This therapeutic approach focuses on how people interpret or think about the world and how their interpretation affects what they do. The therapist is typically quite active in the sessions, almost like a teacher or partner in learning about the depression and what to do about it. People are given homework for the week, and then they discuss the results with their therapist. Typically, therapy takes place once every week or two and lasts for less than a year.

Cognitive-behavioral therapy is based on the idea that thoughts and feelings and behavior are intricately connected. The better people understand these connections, the better they can make changes to improve in all three areas.

Here's an everyday example: two friends, Mariel and Les, are working together in a garden in the springtime. The garden is beautiful, rich with flowers of all different colors and types. A neighbor who is a community leader walks by and quickly says hello, but says nothing about the garden. Mariel thinks, *Hmmm, that neighbor must have a lot on her mind not to appreciate such a beautiful garden,* and then she feels a burst of gratitude that she has room in her heart for flowers. But Les thinks, *I guess this isn't such a great garden after all,* and he starts to feel let down. Carrying this example further, Mariel may dive into her work with renewed vigor, and Les may lose interest.

This is only a moment in two lives. But these moments become who we are. We automatically choose a response to a situation without even being aware of it. And how we respond can greatly affect our way of being in the world.

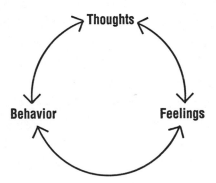

We are a delicate balance of thoughts, feelings, and behavior. When any one of these areas is affected by depression, the other areas are affected too. The purpose of cognitive-behavioral approaches is to help people see how this cycle occurs within them and what they can do to change it. Let's take a look at each part of the cycle as it occurs in depression.

How Does Thinking Affect Depression?

Our attitudes greatly influence how we perceive the events around us and our own experiences. The Talmud says, "We see the world not as it is, but as we are." In other words, we interpret the world differently depending on who we are and how we think about things. When people are experiencing depression, they tend to interpret events in a discouraging way.

Depression clouds and distorts thinking. People with depression usually view their past, present, and future negatively. In turn, the negative thoughts create more depression. It's as if everything is seen through the *opposite* of rose-colored glasses. How many of these thoughts have you had?

Negative evaluation of the past

- I haven't really accomplished anything worthwhile in my life.
- Nothing in my life has gone right.
- Every time I've trusted someone, it's been a disaster.

Negative evaluation of the present

- I'm the type of person who doesn't deserve a break.
- There's no one in my life who would understand.

- I look around me and I can see I have nothing to show for myself.

Negative evaluation of the future

- It's no use trying because nothing will ever turn out right.
- Even if something looks good, I know it won't turn out that way.
- I'm in a hole now and always will be.

If you're depressed, you probably have had many of these thoughts. And you might believe they are true. The irony is that people with depression are not thinking objectively about their situations. This is a symptom of depression, not a character flaw. Often, people who are depressed have trouble stepping outside themselves and seeing that their depression is causing the inaccurate view of their lives. Further, their negative thoughts about themselves and their past, present, and future only serve to fuel the depression.

Sherri's story illustrates what happens with negative thinking. As her depression grew, her thoughts about herself became more and more negative:

I was working as an interior designer and really prided myself on having good ideas. But when I was depressed, I lost all confidence in myself. I didn't think I had anything to offer anyone. Pretty soon I started turning down projects, and when I went to meetings at the office, I didn't say much. When my boss told me they

*were going to have to let me go, I was expecting it; I
wasn't bringing in much revenue and the company
was going through hard times. I felt like a total failure.
I couldn't even think about going to look for a new job.*

It's clear in Sherri's story how each part of the cycle affects the other: negative thoughts lead to withdrawal from new opportunities, which in turn lead to loss of self-esteem and feelings of sadness. Here is what it looks like in the circle diagram.

How Do Feelings Affect Depression?

You might think you're sad because you're depressed, that your depression creates your sadness. But could it be the other way around? Like the old question "Which came first, the chicken or the egg?" it's very difficult to say which came first, the depression or the sadness. This is because they are so intertwined; they fuel each other. The feelings people carry inside build on themselves.

Yes, depression does create sadness, but feelings of sadness might also play a part in maintaining the cycle of depression. To start with, the main feelings of depression are generally sadness, despair, irritability, emptiness, and inadequacy. Delise's feelings were expressed in crying. When she looked back on her depression, she remembered her feelings intensely:

I found myself crying frequently. I felt constantly desperate. My feelings of self-worth were gone. I seemed focused on my worthlessness. I felt suicidal.

But many people with depression find they cannot cry and their feelings are numbed. LaVonda said:

By the end of that year, I felt pretty much defeated and hardly got angry at all anymore—except at work where I was angry before I even arrived. I was mostly just sad—and static.

But even when feelings are numbed, they fuel the depression.

How do feelings affect thinking and behavior? Let's use some parts of these people's stories in the circle diagram to look at how feelings influence other parts of the cycle.

Starting at the point where the feelings occur, you can see how intense sadness can lead to withdrawal and silence, which in turn can lead to feeling more inadequate. In fact, you may have experienced this in times of depression: you feel despair and then withdraw. Family and friends try to "read your signals" and back off. If your withdrawal continues, invitations for social get-togethers stop coming. What

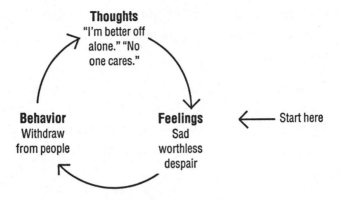

do you think of yourself at that point? Probably less. You might believe, *I am worthless, because no one wants to be with me.* This is a tragic example of how the cycle of depression can affect a person's life.

How Do Actions and Behavior Affect Depression?

Let's take a look at the cycle from one more direction. Behavior is the third part of the cycle that is affected by, and in turn fuels, depression. When people are depressed, it's very difficult for them to behave in ways that might help them feel better. Taking advantage of new opportunities seems almost impossible.

People with depression have trouble actively participating in life. Here are the behaviors that a person with depression is likely to engage in:

- avoiding other people
- getting little or no exercise
- getting stuck in a routine, not going to new places or meeting new people

- getting stuck in minor daily chores and spending more time on them than is usually needed
- sleeping more, or less, than usual

Taken to the extreme, any person—no matter how mentally healthy—engaged only in these behaviors would no doubt develop negative thoughts and feel unhappy.

Here's how it looks in the model we've been using:

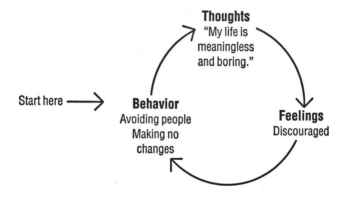

Behavior is a part of the cycle that people can change. Have you heard the slogan *Act as if and the feelings will follow*? This is excellent folk wisdom. Behavior alone can affect people's thoughts and feelings. Sometimes behavior becomes so ingrained and automatic that people have no idea of how it affects the way they view the world and themselves. For example, if every morning you allow only thirty minutes to get up and out the door to be in time for work, no doubt you will start the day feeling irritated and frazzled. Simply getting up fifteen minutes earlier and moving more slowly may create a feeling of calm that lasts throughout the day.

Putting It All Together

The balance of thoughts, feelings, and behavior is like a mobile. When one aspect of a person is affected, all parts react. It can also work like a perpetual-motion machine. As each part of the cycle reacts, it creates energy to set the next part in motion. In real life, no single aspect of a person is affected by itself. At one moment in time, a person may feel emotions, engage in behaviors, and think thoughts that keep the cycle going.

While this picture may seem bleak, there are two avenues of great hope:

- Wherever a person breaks the cycle—be it in thoughts, feelings, or behavior—the positive results "click in" and continue to transform the cycle.
- Even one small change in any part of the cycle can create an ever-growing spiral out of depression.

Let's see how this might work. To break out of the cycle of depression, it's best to work on all three parts of the cycle—thoughts, feelings, and behavior—at the same time. But for clarity, we will consider each area separately.

Changing at the Point of Thoughts

Psychotherapy is one of the best avenues to change thinking. Therapy helps people look at their assumptions, at their thoughts about themselves and their lives. When people tell someone else what their thoughts are, they may see mistakes they never recognized before. Here are other methods that help challenge depressed thinking:

- Read self-help books that encourage new ways of thinking.

- Use daily affirmations to reprogram automatic negative thinking and to experiment with new ways of thinking.

- Engage in daily meditation to find ways to clear the mind of thought.

- Use guided imagery to imagine a different way of being.

All of these methods can affect the way people habitually think. By allowing themselves to have new thoughts, they may find that their cycle of depression changes.

Changing at the Point of Feelings

People can do many simple things every day that have an immediate impact on their feelings. The prescribed actions may not seem logical, but that's okay; feelings are rarely logical. Here are some methods to change everyday life on a feeling level:

- Avoid spending time with people when they are being negative and complaining.

- Rent comedy videos and find other ways to encourage yourself to laugh.

- Look around at your house or office or wherever you spend most of your time. Is it dull and depressing or bright and inviting? (You might need an outside opinion.)

- Get therapeutic massages.

- Read books and magazines that provide you with ways to pamper yourself.

Perhaps these methods seem trite and simplistic. But there is good reason to believe that changing feelings—by changing what you see, how your skin feels, or how often you laugh—can have physiological effects.

Changing at the Point of Actions

Sometimes when people are depressed, they think, *When I'm feeling more energetic, I'll start taking walks or I'll go to the gym and work out or I'll invite my friends over for supper.* But the key out of depression is to start to change the behavior now—to go ahead and participate in life even when you feel you do not have the will to do so.

This is not being phony or false. Rather, it is giving yourself a chance at a "jump start" out of depression. The more new ways of being in the world that people learn, the more likely they are to find the things they need. William Glasser, a noted psychiatrist, says that we have two main needs in life: to love and be loved, and to feel worthwhile to ourselves and others.[4] If we remain isolated and uninvolved in life, there is little chance that we can meet these needs. Here are some changes in behavior that you can try now:

- Go to your usual self-help meetings even if you don't feel like it.
- Start a simple exercise program.
- Set regular hours of sleep and stick to them.
- Keep a journal.

- Paint, draw, or work with clay, and find other creative ways of expressing yourself.
- Read books like *Random Acts of Kindness* to give yourself some ideas for ways to help others. Paradoxically, focusing your attention on other people and acting on their behalf can make you feel better about yourself.

No single change in behavior is going to change your life. But gradually, and over time, a simple change in any one of these areas can have a ripple effect, creating changes in areas you can't predict. The key is to begin, even when you have little faith.

How Do I Find a Therapist?

With all the different approaches to therapy, and the many offices and organizations where you can go to see a therapist, you may feel overwhelmed at the thought of choosing a therapist. You may be thinking, *I don't know how to begin looking for a therapist.* Here are some ways to begin the process.

How to Find Help

As a first step, you may want to think about some practical matters. Ask yourself

- Do you prefer to see a man or a woman?
- How far are you willing to drive on a regular basis?

- How much can you afford to pay?
- Will insurance pay for your therapy?

Once you have answered these questions, you are ready to take the second step—getting names of therapists. The best way to find a therapist is by asking someone you trust for a recommendation. Do you know a friend or relative who has gotten help for depression? Could you ask your physician or clergy person for a referral? How about asking fellow members of a Twelve Step group if they have a recommendation? You could also explore the Internet to locate clinics or counseling centers nearby and learn more about what they might have to offer you. Another way to look for a therapist is to call the state licensing boards of psychiatrists, psychologists, or social workers and ask for a therapist with a specialty of depression. You may also want to check with a state board to learn if there have been any complaints or restrictions placed on the therapist you are considering. (State boards often act as the Better Business Bureaus of professional practice.) Most therapists are very competent and ethical, but you may feel more secure in your choice if you check their records.

The third step is to develop a list of questions that you can use to help you decide if a certain therapist is the right person for you. After you have gathered names of several therapists, you may wish to interview them. It's important to be a smart consumer when searching for a therapist. Therapists know that choosing a therapist is a big step, and most will respect your wish to collect information before making a decision. Many will give you time over the phone or in person, free of charge, to ask these kinds of questions.

Here are the kinds of questions you may wish to include on your list:

- How long has the therapist been in practice?
- What approach does the therapist use in treating depression?
- Is the therapist qualified to provide medications or associated with a psychiatrist who can?
- Is the therapist comfortable and experienced in working with people from a variety of backgrounds and lifestyles? This may be especially important if you have special concerns that you know will play a role in discussions about your life—for instance, if you belong to a minority group or if you are a gay man or lesbian.
- How long does the therapist typically see people for a course of therapy, and how often does the therapist generally schedule appointments?
- If the therapist is away or if an emergency comes up after hours, what arrangements are there for you to get help?

Be sure to take notes during the consultation. And remember that there are no right or wrong answers. But by listening to two or three therapists give their answers and explanations to these questions, you will get a better feel for their approach and how comfortable you may be in working with them.

If you have a very limited selection of therapists because you live in a small community or because your insurance allows you only a few choices, it can still be useful to screen your choices. Because therapy is a very personal process, every therapist will have at least a slightly different way of doing things. Your personal reaction to the therapist is also important. As when you choose a personal physician, you will find that many therapists have similar amounts of knowledge and expertise, but the "chemistry" between you is also important. At the same time, remember that there is no one "best" therapist. Many will be able to help you.

You do not need to choose a therapist right away, and you shouldn't feel pressured by any of them. In fact, allowing yourself a few days to let the conversations settle in your mind may give you the confidence you need to proceed.

Even though it's important to be a careful consumer when choosing a therapist, you might need to choose one without a process of screening. If you are in the midst of a major depressive episode, you may not have the energy or the ability to concentrate that a screening process requires. In this case, you will need to rely more on the recommendation of someone you trust. But you can still ask your therapist some of the same questions even after you've started therapy. However you choose your therapist, step back periodically and ask yourself if you are comfortable and satisfied with the progress you are making. If not, feel free to bring it up with the therapist.

How Not to Find Help

Some people simply go to their family doctors, tell them that they are depressed, and obtain a prescription for antidepressants. They do not see anyone for psychotherapy.

They return to their physician periodically, perhaps every two to three months, for a brief check on a few symptoms of depression and for a refill. Even with the best of general physicians, what's wrong with this approach?

- Without a thorough assessment, you can't be sure the problem is depression. An incorrect diagnosis can delay appropriate treatment.
- Medication might not be the answer.
- Medication alone will not help you discover and address any underlying problems that may be causing or perpetuating the depression.
- You may not get the best medication for your particular problem. Nonspecialists may not be familiar and experienced with all types of medication. They may be giving you what their clinic recommends as standard, or what they are most familiar with, rather than what may work best for you.

Unfortunately, with the growing trend in managed health care, the practice of prescribing antidepressants without thorough assessment and referral to psychotherapy is increasing. Depression is complex. It can be a lifelong, debilitating disease, and you owe it to yourself to get the most thorough treatment available. Research has shown that depressed people are less likely than other people to switch health care plans when they are dissatisfied with the care they are receiving.[5] Don't let yourself be one of them!

Is Psychotherapy Working?
Patterns of Change in Therapy

Once you have chosen a therapist and started the work of psychotherapy, you may wonder from time to time if it is working. This is an important question and one you should pay attention to. As you assess your therapy, remember that psychotherapy can be a lot of work; it takes time, and the results are not always easy to see along the way.

People experiencing dysthymia should know that this ongoing, low-level form of depression can take longer to treat than major depression. If people are predisposed to having low moods, this pattern will not change quickly or easily. Still, over time, the dysthymia can lessen. And therapy may help people live full and relatively contented lives even while they are experiencing dysthymia.

But with any depression, change doesn't happen all at once or quickly. People might go for a while without seeing any changes—and then go for a stretch where everything seems new. Sometimes people feel discouraged because they find themselves repeating old patterns that they thought were behind them. But there is some predictability to the way change occurs in therapy, and knowing this may help to keep people from feeling discouraged. It also may help people evaluate their therapy.

A group of researchers at the University of Rhode Island and the University of Houston has found a pattern to the changes people make in therapy.[6] Based on their research, they have designed a model with five phases.

Precontemplation Phase

During the precontemplation phase, people don't recognize that there is a problem or a need for change, even though others may see it. Someone in this phase may think, *My boss and my wife are the source of my problems*, or, *It's better to just cope with problems than to try to change them.*

Contemplation Phase

In the contemplation phase, people are aware that there is a problem, but they aren't quite ready to do something about it. At this stage, a person might wonder, *Who would I go see for help?* Or, *Would therapy do any good?* They are starting to realize that they are depressed, that their low feelings are not just a passing mood. In this phase, a person might think, *Perhaps it would be worthwhile to work on my problems*, or, *Maybe someone will be able to help me.*

Preparation Phase

People in the preparation phase are making a commitment to do something to help themselves. They might be asking others for their recommendations about a therapist or calling local agencies or clinics. They might call their insurance company to find out what's covered and what providers they can choose from their insurance plan. They might call a few therapists to ask them questions about how they treat depression or how much they charge. In this phase, a person might think things like, *I believe I have problems and I want to work on them.*

Action Phase

When people are in the action phase, they're working hard to make changes. They are in therapy, and they are trying out new ways of thinking, new ways of acting. In general, they are taking risks that they wouldn't have taken before. This is the phase in which a person might say with deserved pride, *Anyone can talk about changing; I'm actually doing something about it.* During this phase, people might keep things around as a reminder not to give in to their problems—poems or slogans, for instance. They might make new friends who are supportive of their efforts. They might keep a journal, draw, or find other ways to express how they are changing.

Maintenance Phase

Some people don't recognize the importance of the maintenance phase, or even the fact that it exists. In this phase, people need to continue consciously putting into practice all the changes they have made in the action stage. They might find these things happening naturally—maintaining friendships with supportive people, keeping up a program of physical activity. They're now more aware of the need to nurture themselves when they've had a hard day, instead of slipping into depressive thought and feelings. They recognize that old feelings and old patterns of behavior may come back and tap them on the shoulder, but they know now that they can let them go.

In reality, people don't go through these phases one by one. As they are making progress in one area of life, they might just be starting to realize a need to change another area. Or they find themselves revisiting their commitment to work on certain problems. This is all natural and part of the continuous pattern of change in therapy. The diagram below shows one way to visualize it.[7]

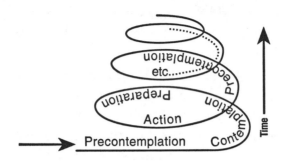

As the spiral shows, therapy is not a straight, steady line of changes. It isn't always smooth, and sometimes it feels as if it goes backward before it goes forward again. People might even wonder, *Is it really worth it?*

If depression is a signal that a person's life is out of balance and that something inside needs to be changed, therapy can help people see where the changes need to occur. Therapy gives people the time and support to make those changes. They can learn what helps them move further from depression and even learn how to prevent themselves from slipping into similar episodes in the future. Sometimes depression cannot be prevented, but therapy can help people see the warning signs and get help before they are consumed by it.

What If I Am Recovering from Addiction?

Depression isn't just being sad; depression also shows up in negative thinking. People who are depressed and in a Twelve Step program may notice that they are becoming cynical, doubting the power of recovery tools that worked for them in the past. They may start to skip their daily meditation and inventory, or skip the meetings they used to find helpful, thinking, *What's the use? They don't really do any good.* When they do go to meetings or see recovering friends, they may find themselves thinking about them in negative, critical ways: *That sponsor of mine is just a bag of wind; he doesn't really know anything,* or, *If Sally says one more time that she's grateful about something, I'm going to just walk out.* They may struggle with daydreams about using or drinking as an escape. When they think about the fact that chemicals won't help, they may think about suicide. The more distorted and negative their thinking is, the more they withdraw and the more unhappy they become.

Karan looked back on her time of depression:

> *I felt guilty and didn't want to tell anyone how I felt. I felt like a phony, that all that good Alcoholics Anonymous stuff I was spouting was a lie because I was feeling so miserable. And I was ashamed. I thought I wasn't working a good enough program. I was also afraid that if I shared my feelings openly, I'd discourage a newcomer to AA.*

The more Karan mulled over these thoughts, the more sad and inadequate she felt. In the circle diagram, Karan's process of thinking and feeling looks like this:

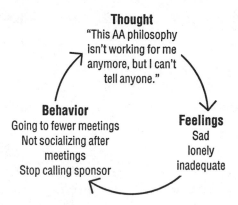

Thought
"This AA philosophy isn't working for me anymore, but I can't tell anyone."

Feelings
Sad
lonely
inadequate

Behavior
Going to fewer meetings
Not socializing after meetings
Stop calling sponsor

Karan got help, but it's easy to imagine how this cycle can lead to a relapse to chemical use.

What Does This Mean for Me?

Depression has a tremendous impact on your thoughts, feelings, and behavior. You can feel truly handicapped in coping with the world when you are depressed. But through therapy, you can change. You may prefer one therapeutic approach over another depending on your learning style, the way you think about things, and the way you go about making changes in your life. Regardless of the approach you choose, effective treatment is possible.

Further Questions

How long does therapy take?

There is no standard time frame for therapy. Most people begin to feel better within a few months, and most can see significant changes in less than a year. But according to the nature of your issues and how long you have built patterns around them, you may need more or less time.

These days, the amount of time people tend to spend in therapy is generally decreasing, and many see a therapist for only a few weeks or a few months. There is a growing trend toward a "brief therapy" model. When therapists use a brief therapy model, they take a very active role in teaching you about your depression and how to begin making changes in your life. Therapy may last only six to twelve sessions over the course of three or four months. The idea is to give you a burst of intensive help that can see you through on your own. Appointments may be built in for later dates, either as booster sessions or as a safety net to handle stressful times.

This trend toward brief therapy is due in part to the growing awareness that, for some people, much can be accomplished in a short time. It is also due in part to today's political climate—the emphasis in the United States on providing good health care at the lowest cost. Of course, brief therapy is not suitable for everyone. The amount of time you need to spend in therapy depends on the nature of your depression and the unique circumstances in your life.

How often do people go to therapy?

Some people begin by seeing a therapist quite frequently, perhaps every week. As improvement begins, they reduce the frequency to once every two to three weeks.

Do I have to understand the root cause of my depression before I can get better?

Understanding yourself is a lifelong process and you cannot gather all the insight you need in one course of psychotherapy. That doesn't mean you can't make progress and find ways to climb out of depression. In fact, it is sometimes only later, when you are stronger and on stable ground, that you can begin to fully understand the nature of your depression.

How do medications and psychotherapy fit together?

Antidepressant medications are intended to be used in conjunction with psychotherapy. Many people with depression are able to benefit from psychotherapy alone, without medication. But others need medication as well.

Often when people are using both kinds of treatments, therapy and medication, they see both a psychotherapist and a psychiatrist. They meet with a therapist relatively frequently, once every week or two, to gain a greater understanding of their depression and to learn how to manage or improve their symptoms. They meet with a psychiatrist less frequently to have medication prescribed or adjusted. Ideally, all three people—the patient, the psychotherapist, and the psychiatrist—work together, exchanging information as treatment continues. Often people can stop taking the antidepressant as their depression lifts, but they continue seeing the therapist to deepen their understanding of themselves and their depression. Some psychiatrists play both roles—providing psychotherapy and prescribing medications—though this is becoming less common.

You may wish to discuss the question of medication with your psychotherapist. To learn more about anti-depressant medication, see chapter 7.

What Can I Do to Help Myself?

1. Do you know anyone who is in psychotherapy? If you wanted to learn more about what psycho-therapy is like, could you ask this person some questions? Does this person find therapy help-ful? In what ways? You do not need to tell this person that you are thinking of trying psycho-therapy if it does not feel safe to do so. Another way to learn more about psychotherapy is to do some exploring on the Internet.

2. What types of therapists are available in your community? Look in your phone book and start exploring. Is there a local mental health associa-tion or a chapter of the National Alliance for the Mentally Ill? Call your state psychological asso-ciation or state psychiatric association to find out what kind of referral information they can give you.

3. Does your community have a local hot line for emotional problems? Sometimes talking to a stranger about your depression is good practice. You can begin to find words to describe what you are experiencing. And you can learn that people will accept you and listen to you.

Chapter 6

What Can I Do about My Depression? Lifestyle

When I'm depressed I don't care. I eat the wrong things. I don't take care of myself.

∽ Nora

For most people, lifestyle changes alone will not erase depression. But changing the way we live can lay a good foundation for recovery from depression to occur. In this chapter, we'll take a look at several components of everyday life and how they relate to depression.

How Can My Lifestyle Affect My Depression?

Relationships

Good relationships may be a protective factor in the development or recurrence of depression. We know that there is a strong connection between depression and unhappy marriages, but it might not be immediately obvious what causes what. Certainly living with a depressed person can cause a strain in the relationship. But there's now evidence that there is a strong causal relationship in the other direction. For example:

- In one study, women whose mothers died in their childhood were less likely to develop depression if they were married to a man who provided high levels of affection.[1]

- One long-term study found that women in supportive relationships were much more likely to recover from depression than those in conflictual relationships. It should be pointed out here that while research is typically done on traditional marriages, the results can be generalized to other long-term stable relationships.

If it is true that supportive, confidential, loving relationships help depression recovery, what can a person do? One researcher and therapist, Dr. J. M. Lewis noted three types of destructive relationships common in depression:[2]

1. A dominant-submissive relationship, where one person (usually the woman) has only a small voice in the relationship. The other person is emotionally distant, controlling, and seems not to care about the relationship.

2. Both partners are distant in the relationship. Prior to the onset of depression, someone else in the family—usually a child—provided the basis for intimacy. The child may die or grow up and leave home, leaving two adults with little basis for their own relationship.

3. Both partners are in constant conflict. In this type of relationship, the depression may be a reaction against the conflict or an attempt to gain some control in the relationship.

All of these patterns of interacting can change. New ways of relating can be learned and a new relationship developed. Change occurs best in family or marital counseling, where both people in the relationship can be open, vulnerable, and accept feedback. What is the goal in therapy? Dr. Lewis, again, lays out six themes of well-functioning marriages:

1. Shared power.
   Positive examples: Leona and Joshua decide together where the family vacation will be this year. Marty and Ree decide together on a family budget and share responsibility to make it work.
   Negative examples: The family always goes on vacations to the places Mom's or Dad's business conferences are being held. One person handles the money and tells the family how they will spend it.

2. High levels of both connectedness and separation.
   Positive example: Jamie and Eric share many of the same passions—they enjoy the same type of music and love to dance. But they are miles apart in their political beliefs: Jamie is a Republican and Eric is a Democrat. They each respect the other person's point of view and the time

they each take with their respective grassroots groups.

Negative example: A couple thinks something is wrong when they have different opinions and interests. One person generally defines the interest and the other goes along with it. After a while, they always "agree on everything."

3. Respect for each other's own reality as true.
Positive example: Reeve refuses to have a natural Christmas tree because he hates to clean up the needles when it dies and has to be taken down. Cari can't imagine having an artificial tree, as she grew up with real Christmas trees that her family chopped down in the woods. After a day of arguing, they agreed to accept each other's reality—and bought a small potted Norway pine.
Negative example: One partner decides the other's reality is wrong, misguided, narrow, or just plain stupid, and continues the argument.

4. Open expression of emotion.
Positive example: In Ivy and Paul's marriage, it's okay for both of them to cry, to admit feeling hurt, and to ask for comfort.
Negative example: In some relationships, the only messages that are valued are logical facts, well-stated points of view, and articulate positions.

5. Strong mutual problem solving.
Positive example: When their daughter ran away, Mikelle and Gary worked together to figure out

what to do, who to contact, and the best way to keep her safe and get her back home.

Negative example: Tragedy is something that either brings couples together or tears them apart. In some relationships, one person blames the other, takes over to "solve" the problem, or just leaves.

6. When conflict occurs, it doesn't get magnified and is resolved.

   Positive example: Dan and Esther have been married long enough—and have worked hard enough on their relationship—to know how to state their disagreement, stick to the topic, and get it settled before it gets blown out of proportion.

   Negative example: Some partners don't learn "fair fighting" and even small disagreements build, getting added to the pile of all the old, unresolved small arguments. Both people end up stuck in a morass of hurt and anger.

What can you do about everyday relationships with friends and family? When you're depressed, you may feel more like withdrawing than socializing. Or you might feel both things at once—a yearning to be with other people *and* a wish to be alone. Here's how Edie talked about her ambivalence:

When I'm in the middle of my depression, I want to be left alone. But I also appreciate it when people tell me they're there for me and at least invite me to come along with them. Even though I might say no, I like to be included.

Isolation makes a depression worse. Even when you don't see the point of it and don't have much to contribute, it's generally best to spend time with other people. Instead of eating lunch by yourself in your office, go sit in the company dining room near your colleagues. Instead of taking that walk by yourself, call a few friends and ask if they'd like to come along with you. Each attempt at making contact with other people adds a thread to a tapestry that can support you through your depression.

Learned Optimism

Do you assume things will always go badly for you? Do you feel you will never have the luck, talent, skill, brains, poise, or whatever else you think you might need to be happy or successful? While self-doubt is a common symptom of depression, some people adopt this attributional style as a lifelong pattern. Pessimists are people who believe that bad events will last a long time, will undermine everything they do, and are their own fault.[3] Optimists, on the other hand, are more likely to see bad events as isolated incidents that will have a limited effect and are due to fate or someone else's fault. Our tendencies toward chronic pessimism or optimism can play a huge role in the way life rolls out for us.

Dr. Martin Seligman, who has studied and written about optimism for decades has found that optimists are more likely to accomplish their goals, be happier, be healthier, and live longer than pessimists.[4] Though it takes practice and may seem unnatural to someone entrenched in pessimism, it is possible to become an optimist. A good place to start is by reviewing the section on changing your thinking in chapter 5 (pages 109–110) of this book. Seligman's book *Learned Optimism* provides a step-by-step guide for crossing the divide between pessimism and optimism.

Light

For people who live in northern climates, sunlight is hard to come by during the winter months. As humans, we seem to have a biological requirement for natural light. Special light boxes have been invented to simulate natural light. These have shown in study after study to produce quite remarkable results in people with seasonal affective disorder (SAD). In several studies, 50 to 75 percent of people with SAD experience a significant decrease in their depression when they undergo light therapy.[5] While improvement is quite dramatic, people may not feel as completely free of depressive symptoms as they do in the summertime, when there is natural sunlight.[6]

Light boxes can purchased in specialized stores or via the Internet. Best results seem to occur with boxes at 10,000 lux (a level of brightness) when used for two weeks or longer. Some people have initial minor side effects, such as headaches or vision problems, which disappear within four to five days of using the light box.[7]

Surprisingly, light therapy has shown promising results with other disorders as well. A study at the University of California at San Diego found that light therapy significantly decreases depressive symptoms in nonseasonal depression, that is, regular major depressive disorders.[8] And the turnaround begins much sooner than with antidepressants—within a week. These researchers suggest that a combined approach of light therapy with anti-depressants might be most beneficial. Light therapy may also be helpful for people with eating disorders (especially for those whose binge-purge cycle is worse in the fall and winter), premenstrual disorders, and some sleep disorders.

Seasonal disorders and light therapy have gained such recognition that a special office has been established in the National Institutes of Health. Dr. Thomas Wehr, head of the Section Biological Rhythms of the National Institute of Mental Health, has stated, "Light therapy is one of the most successful and practical results of basic research in biological rhythms."[9]

You might be wondering, *What's the magic? How does the light box work?* It is known that melatonin, one of the body's natural hormones, is secreted at night and stops in the morning with the arrival of daylight. However, for people living in climates with extreme darkness, there is no early morning daylight to signal the pineal gland to stop producing melatonin. The light box, used in the morning, provides this signal.[10]

For anyone who is depressed or prone to depression, it's a good idea to get as much natural sunlight as possible during the fall and winter months. Even taking a short walk outside at lunchtime might be enough to keep biological systems balanced. If this isn't possible, getting a light box is a great investment. In fact, many health insurance policies will pay for light boxes. Using the lights for thirty minutes each morning seems to be the best method, rather than using it in the evening. Many people even read or watch TV while using the light box.

Exercise

Physical activity helps improve overall mood. During exercise, feelings of sadness, anxiety, and anger decrease. After exercise, overall mood is improved, as well as self-concept and self-esteem.[11] Surprisingly, increased exercise is also correlated with improvements in overall level of optimism.[12]

You might think, *Sure, if I were in great shape, I'd feel good about myself and my life too!* But it's not the physical condition of a person that makes a difference. It's the physical activity itself. Simple running, walking, swimming, skiing, or participating in any other activity that moves the large muscle groups produces a positive overall effect on mental health.[13]

We know now, too, that physical exercise not only improves overall mood, but acts as an antidepressant for people who are moderately depressed. Numerous studies have shown that a prescription for exercise is effective in reducing symptoms of depression and anxiety in clinical populations. The International Society of Sports Psychology recommends using physical activity as an adjunct to other forms of treatment for depression.[14] A recent study by researchers at Duke University bears this out. They randomly assigned a group of 156 middle-aged depressed adults into one of three groups: exercise, medication (Zoloft), or a combination of medication plus exercise. At the end of sixteen weeks, between 60 and 70 percent of people in all three groups were significantly improved, to the point that they no longer met diagnostic criteria for depression. In other words, *exercise alone produced the same effect as an antidepressant.* The improvement in symptoms was faster for the antidepressant group, but at sixteen weeks, there was no difference. The researchers concluded that a "brisk 30 minute walk or jog around the track three times a week may be just as effective in relieving the symptoms of major depression as the standard treatment of antidepressant medication"—which is quite a revolutionary statement.[15]

There are several theories about how exercise might produce changes in mood, including the possibility that exercise increases brain levels of important neurotransmitters, such as serotonin.

Even as you read this, you might be thinking, *An exercise program wouldn't help me. In fact, when I do try to follow an exercise program, I can't. And that's just one more thing for me to beat myself up about.* Or, you may have had bad experiences with exercise, resulting in injury or frustration. But the program that's needed is really quite simple—just thirty minutes, three times a week.

Some people make the mistake of thinking, *Well, if thirty minutes is good, I'll do forty-five minutes,* or, *I'll really do this right—I'll exercise every day.* In fact, starting an exercise program at an intense level or increasing the level too quickly is a prescription for failure. The best method is to start at a low but perfectly adequate level and either keep it there or increase it in length or intensity only 10 percent per month. This way your body (and probably your schedule) slowly adapts to the biochemical and muscular changes that are occurring. If you increase your workouts too fast, you may get sick, become overly fatigued, and become unable to sustain a program for a very long period of time.[16]

Eating Right

There's no sure diet to cure depression. But some intriguing research findings give us some clues about what kind of food might be helpful or harmful.

The Tryptophan Deficiency Theory

Tryptophan is an amino acid that is a common part of our biological makeup. When tryptophan levels decline, serotonin levels in the brain also decline. Based on our knowledge of how antidepressants work, we know that low serotonin levels are associated with depression. So it makes sense to wonder if low levels of tryptophan in our diets contribute to depression.

Numerous studies have been done to explore this link.[17] Research with animals has demonstrated that serotonin levels in the brain fall when animals are fed a diet devoid of tryptophan. Research with humans has found that tryptophan depletion results in lowered mood in normal people. In depressed people who are on antidepressants, tryptophan depletion causes the depressive symptoms to return quickly, sometimes within just five to seven hours. In normal people with a family history of depression, tryptophan depletion significantly lowers mood, compared with normal people with no family history of depression. This suggests that there may be a biological basis to tryptophan depletion sensitivity.

Carbohydrates help tryptophan enter the brain. Carbohydrates are food such as rice, pasta, bread, potatoes, corn, and oats.[18]

Folic Acid Deficiency Theory

Folic acid is part of a cycle involving two important natural body chemicals that regulate mood: serotonin and S-adenosylmethionine (SAM-e). Decreases in folic acid can result in decreased SAM-e and decreased serotonin. In at least two studies, administration of folic acid in patients with affective disorders resulted in improvement. In one study, people with bipolar illness on lithium who also took folic acid did significantly better after one year than people with bipolar illness participating in the study who took a placebo with their lithium.[19]

Folates, or folic acid, are vitamins found in natural foods like green, leafy vegetables (spinach and lettuce) and in fresh fruits (apples and oranges). It's rare to have a deficiency in these vitamins, as they are so common. But with their loss of appetite, depressed people may become deficient. Most daily multivitamins contain the needed amount of folic acid if a normal level cannot be sustained by a routine diet.[20]

Omega-3 Fats

Omega-3 fat is a natural compound in certain cell membranes of all healthy people. Omega-3 fats are found in fish, especially salmon, mackerel, and herring. One study found that depressed people have levels of omega-3 fat that are 40 percent lower than those of normal people.[21] It's hard to know what causes what, but one theory is that omega-3 deficiencies may make a person more vulnerable to depression.

Deficiencies may also make depressed people more vulnerable to relapse. Researchers at Harvard and Baylor studied the effect of omega-3 fatty acids on the course of bipolar illness. Thirty people with bipolar disorder received a pill containing omega-3 or a placebo in addition to their regular medication. At the end of four months, the people in the omega-3 group were doing significantly better than they had been before. Their disease was more stable, and they reported a more stable mood. One theory is that omega-3 fatty acids are involved in signal transduction in important neurological pathways, similar to how lithium and other mood stabilizers work.[22]

With all of these compounds—tryptophan, folates, and omega-3 acids—research on their effect on depression is so new and controversial that there are no guidelines about how much people should get in their diets. But research findings do suggest that an important relationship exists between the food we eat and our state of mind.

Further Questions

I'm in no mood to exercise. Wouldn't it be better to wait until my depression lifts?

When you're depressed, you may have very little energy, and it seems crazy to spend it on something like intentional exercise. But, paradoxically, expending energy can create more energy. The best thing you can do for yourself might be to take a walk, a run, or a bike ride, or do some other easy form of activity.

You hear so much about diets and healthy food. I can't keep it all straight. Is there a proven healthy diet?

There is no one diet that is best. Nutritional researchers disagree about lots of aspects of diet, but all agree that a balanced one is important. When you're depressed, you might not be getting enough food. Or maybe you are eating from a very narrow band of foods—the same old things every day. The best thing you might be able to do for your body while you are depressed is to eat a variety of foods and take a daily multivitamin.

What Can I Do to Help Myself?

Many people who seek help for depression lead frantic, overscheduled lives, with little room for sleep. Here are some daily things anyone can do to lay a foundation for recovery from depression. You may still need medication or months of psychotherapy to get through your depression, but adopting these lifestyle changes will give you a better chance of recovery.

1. Set a regular schedule and stick to it. Realistically, you might not be able to schedule every day—but look for ways you can make your time more predictable and less chaotic.

2. Go to bed and get up at the same time every day. Even if you can't sleep, try to keep yourself on a regular bedtime schedule. Your body will catch up with you and adjust. There's even a name for this: sleep hygiene.

3. Build in calming rituals—even small ones—that you can do every day. These might include lighting a candle at the end of the day, setting aside twenty minutes to listen to music, or stopping by a coffeehouse for a cup of tea or decaffeinated coffee.

4. Schedule one event with a friend every week. Although you may want to isolate yourself, resist the temptation. Even if you don't feel like it, make sure to plan one activity that would normally be fun and do it with other people. This might include going skiing on a Saturday morning, taking a long walk, visiting a museum, or seeing a movie.

5. Say no to extra demands on your schedule. Know your priorities and stick with them. When you are depressed, one of your priorities is keeping a simple schedule.

6. Exercise for twenty to thirty minutes at least three times a week. This doesn't have to mean a membership to a trendy fitness center, and you don't have to begin training for a marathon. It's simply a matter of telling yourself that getting exercise is just as important for you as getting insulin is for a diabetic.

7. Stop eating potato chips, candy, caffeine, and other junk food that isn't good for you. Eat a balanced diet of more natural foods. If you need help structuring a balanced diet, consult with a nutritionist. If you're not ready to do that, check out *nutrition* on your computer's Internet search engine and get some ideas about better eating. You may not decide to become a vegetarian or adopt the latest health-food diet, but there are enduring, practical things you can do, starting today, to give your body better fuel.

Chapter 7

What Can I Do about My Depression? Antidepressant Medication

Taking antidepressants does not solve my problems, but gives me the strength to tackle the problems. It puts a floor under me below which I cannot sink. The floor, for the first time in my life, is the same as everybody else's floor.

      ~ Raul, who has dysthymia and periodic bouts of major depression

Depression is not just an illness of the mind or the spirit. Depression is also an illness of the body. When people are depressed, the neurotransmitters—the chemicals that carry messages between the nerve cells in the brain—may be affected. It isn't clear whether the chemical changes cause the depression or whether the depression causes the chemical changes; it may be different for different people. Regardless, medications that affect the neurotransmitters can be very important in bringing relief from depression.

People who are depressed may have many questions as they consider using antidepressants:

- What is antidepressant medication?
- How do I decide to use antidepressant medication?
- What is it like to take antidepressant medication?
- What are the side effects of antidepressant medication?
- When and how do I stop taking antidepressant medication?

What Is Antidepressant Medication?

Antidepressants are medications that may help lift some of the darkness of depression. (Remember that depression includes a whole constellation of symptoms, not just feeling blue.) Antidepressants can take away some of the low mood and relieve the physical symptoms of depression, such as sleep disruptions, appetite changes, and inability to concentrate. It's important to realize that antidepressants are not "uppers"; they don't make people happy or cheerful. And unlike uppers, antidepressants are not addictive. In the following pages, we will review the main types of antidepressants and explain how they work.

There are five main categories of antidepressants: *monoamine oxidase inhibitors* (MAO inhibitors or MAOIs), *tricyclics, selective serotonin re-uptake inhibitors* (SSRIs), *unique antidepressants,* and *mood stabilizers.* We will begin with the older antidepressants.

Monoamine Oxidase Inhibitors

Monoamine oxidase inhibitors (MAOIs) include the drugs Parnate, Nardil, and Marplan. Originally developed to treat tuberculosis, MAOIs were also found to help alleviate depression among people who had both tuberculosis and depression. Since then, more effective drugs have been developed to treat tuberculosis. Drugs more effective in the treatment of most depressions have also been developed. However, since newer antidepressants aren't effective for every person, monoamine oxidase inhibitors are still used to treat depression that does not respond to other drugs.

How MAOIs Work

Monoamine oxidase inhibitors work by doing just what their name says they do: they stop the action of an enzyme called *monoamine oxidase*. Monoamine oxidase breaks down some important neurotransmitters in the brain called *amines*. Amines include several neurotransmitters: serotonin, epinephrine, norepinephrine, and dopamine. Usually the monoamine oxidase enzyme is needed because neurotransmitters need to be broken down in their own life cycle. However, according to the amine theory of depression, people who are depressed need all the amine neurotransmitters they can get. If oxidase is inhibited or stopped, more amines will be available in the brain.

Neurochemistry is difficult to follow, so here's an analogy that should make it a little easier to understand. Imagine you live in a house where you can toss your cardboard boxes down the stairs and someone magically flattens them and sends them out the back door for recycling.

This system works so well, you never think twice about it. Then one day, you are packing for a big move and you need all the boxes you can get. As you toss them down the stairs, you say, "Save this box!" But the person at the bottom of the stairs knows how to do just one thing—flatten boxes. One solution is to send down a specialist, someone who can stop the box flattener so the boxes can be saved for your use.

In this analogy, the boxes are the special neurotransmitters called amines. They start out whole, but are hurled across a space (in the brain, it's called a synapse) from one cell to another. Usually, the neurotransmitters need to be broken down. But in the case of depression, they're needed in their full form a while longer. To make sure this happens, an inhibitor is sent in to prevent them from being broken down.

Side Effects and Other Problems

MAOIs are not "first line" (the first recommended) antidepressants because of potential problems associated with their use. Physicians generally prescribe them only after other antidepressants have been tried. The main problem is that people taking MAOIs cannot eat or drink anything that contains the monoamine called *tyramine*. And tyramine is found in many common foods and beverages, including aged cheeses, yogurt, canned food, alcohol, caffeine, and chocolate. Since the medication MAOI doesn't differentiate between what kinds of amines it allows to build up, tyramine builds up in the body if a person consumes these foods or beverages. Tyramine affects blood pressure. If a person's tyramine levels increase too much, blood pressure can suddenly increase, which in its most extreme state can cause death.

Despite their risks, MAOIs are effective antidepressants for many people. If other antidepressants have not worked, MAOIs may be prescribed, and people taking them must simply limit their diets. Their doctor can provide them with a comprehensive list of foods to avoid.

Note that because of the relatively low margin of safety with these drugs, they are generally not prescribed for addicts, who may be at risk for relapse to alcohol or other drug use.

Tricyclics

Tricyclics were first developed in the late 1950s and early 1960s. Common names of the different types of tricyclics include Tofranil, Elavil, Asendin, Aventyl, and Sinequan. Norpramin (desipramine) is a later version. Tricyclics produce many therapeutic effects, including improved appetite, sleep, and mood. It generally takes two to four weeks before these medications begin to take effect. People may feel sedated and sleepy before they begin to experience the benefits of the drug. Research generally shows high success rates with tricyclics; 60 to 70 percent of people who are depressed improve with tricyclics.

How Tricyclics Work

Tricyclic antidepressants work by blocking the re-uptake of various neurotransmitters in the brain, especially serotonin and norepinephrine. Theorists believe that a certain amount of these neurotransmitters is needed in the synapses between the cells. If the amount becomes too low, the theory goes, depression occurs. Blocking their re-uptake ensures that more of the neurotransmitter will be available between the cells.

As an analogy, imagine a game in which the object is to keep at least forty basketballs in motion. A thrower tosses basketballs into the middle of a gym. Some of the balls are red, some blue, some green, and some yellow. A catcher grabs the balls and puts them in baskets. There are extra points for keeping the blue and red balls in motion. But pretty soon, hardly any balls are left in the open area of the gym! No matter how hard the thrower works, the ball catcher is never far behind.

In this analogy, the thrower and catcher are special cells in the brain—*neurons*—that are responsible for transporting the neurotransmitters. The basketballs are the different kinds of neurotransmitters, and the red and blue balls are norepinephrine and serotonin. One solution is for the thrower to hire someone else to come into the gym and stop the ball catcher from picking up so many balls, especially the red and blue balls. This will keep more of them in motion. Theorists believe that tricyclics serve this function. They block the re-uptake of neurotransmitters, especially norepinephrine and serotonin.

Side Effects and Other Problems

Tricyclics have one major downfall: their side effects. These include dry mouth, urinary retention, constipation, drowsiness, fast heart rate, and dizziness when standing up quickly (which happens because blood pressure drops too quickly). In addition, sexual desire and performance may be diminished. Many people are able to live with the side effects; for other people, the side effects are extreme or intolerable. These people may not be able to experience the benefits of tricyclics because they stop taking the drug or they take it in lower doses than are recommended.

The negative side effects of antidepressants have been a significant problem for a long time. The search is on for an antidepressant without such side effects. The first drug of that kind is Prozac, one of a new family of antidepressants called *selective serotonin re-uptake inhibitors.*

Selective Serotonin Re-uptake Inhibitors

The public's thinking about depression and antidepressants has been revolutionized by the selective serotonin re-uptake inhibitors (SSRIs), including Prozac, Zoloft, Paxil, Luvox, and Celexa. In 1987, Prozac became the first in this family to be approved by the Food and Drug Administration. The SSRIs are now well-accepted in the medical field and general public, and used as "first line" antidepressants. That is, these are the antidepressants that are likely to be tried first when a person goes to a physician for help with depression. The SSRIs are preferred because they have fewer side effects, have low overdose potential, and are easy to use, often requiring only one dose a day. Some people think that the success of SSRIs has to do with their superior effectiveness. Surprisingly, this is not a factor; about 67 percent of people taking any antidepressant, an SSRI or another type, will experience improvement.[1] However, the SSRIs are so well-tolerated by most people that more people are finding relief from their depression by taking them. This became big news and has revolution-ized the way depression is treated.

How SSRIs work

One characteristic of serotonin re-uptake inhibitors sets them apart from all other antidepressants: SSRIs primarily block the re-uptake of only *one* of the brain's neurotrans-mitters, serotonin. That is why they are called "selective" re-uptake inhibitors. SSRIs work by maintaining the nat-ural level of serotonin between cells of the brain. In this way they are very "clean"; they affect only serotonin. The other antidepressants—tricyclics and MAOIs—affect other brain chemicals in addition to serotonin. Why does this matter? It seems that the more specific the action on the neurotransmitters, the fewer the side effects. The fewer the side effects, the easier antidepressants are for people to take. SSRIs must generally be taken for about ten days to three weeks before they become effective.[2]

Side Effects and Other Problems

People tend to have less trouble with SSRIs than with other antidepressants. Still, some people do experience side ef-fects. These can include nausea or diarrhea, abdominal dis-tress, headaches, nervousness, and sleep problems. More recently, since the SSRIs have become widely marketed and used, another important side effect has become apparent: many people who take SSRIs have difficulty with sexual functioning. The number of these problems may be under-reported for several reasons: (1) problems caused by the an-tidepressant may be attributed to the depressive disorder (which may or may not be true), (2) people are reluctant to talk with their physicians about specifics of their sexual behavior or difficulties, and (3) some of the effects on sexual function are quite subtle. The most typical sexual problems reported are delayed or absent ejaculation in men or delayed or absent orgasm in women. Paroxetine has received the most reports of sexual functioning side effects. During early treatment, when depressive symptoms are still evident, the inability to engage in sex may not be a problem, as depression itself usually causes loss of interest. However, as time goes on and the depression lifts, sexual dysfunction is less likely to be an acceptable side effect. The following are recommended techniques for dealing with sexual dysfunction, in partnership with a physician:[3]

- Give it time. Tolerance to the medication may develop, and the sexual dysfunction side effect may abate, along with other side effects.
- Reduce the dose. Many of the sexual dysfunction problems seem to be dose-related. If the overall depression can be managed at a lower dosage level, it may be that sexual function problems will decrease at a lower dose.
- Take a "drug holiday." For most of the medications, sexual dysfunction is reversed within one to three days after withdrawal of the medication. Prozac is an exception, taking one to three weeks. However, a host of other unwanted symptoms may appear as part of a drug discontinuation syndrome, so this may not be a viable option.
- Change to a different, non-SSRI antidepressant, such as Wellbutrin, Serzone, or Remeron.

- Add a different medication that boosts sexual performance or counters the antidepressant medication's side effect. This method is generally not desirable, as there are no studies examining the effect of such medication combinations.

Using SSRIs for Other Disorders

The balance of serotonin in the brain may be important for disorders besides depression, including alcoholism, obsessive-compulsive disorder, panic disorder, and eating disorders. Because people who have these problems also often experience depression, physicians may prescribe an SSRI. These medications are apt to help the depression and may also help the other problem.

Unique Antidepressants

There are several newer antidepressants that have been developed, and new ones are being studied every day. The new generation of antidepressants marketed in the United States includes Effexor, Wellbutrin, Remeron, Vestra, Desyrel (and other brands of trazodone), and Serzone. These medications usually act on serotonin, and they have an effect on the uptake or action of other neurotransmitters as well. For example, Remeron, Serzone, and Effexor each increase the amount of serotonin and norepinephrine (another neurotransmitter) in the brain's synapses, but in different ways.

The advantage of some of the newer antidepressants is that they either have fewer side effects or the types of side effects are more tolerable. For example, Wellbutrin,

Serzone, and Remeron are reported to have less effect on sexual functioning that most of the SSRIs.

Mood Stabilizers

Special medications are used for treating bipolar disorders. These include lithium and anticonvulsants such as Tegretol or Depakote. Often, they may be prescribed together, particularly if a person experiences rapid changes in cycles or mood states. The method of action for antimanic medications is generally not known. But as many as 40 to 60 percent of people with bipolar illness can be stabilized on lithium, the oldest antimanic drug, alone. The effectiveness of lithium may be decreasing over the decades, which is a concern. There is some indication that going off and on lithium may create a state where lithium loses its effectiveness, and use of antidepressants may induce cycling or, again, make a person's body less able to respond to lithium.[4]

Mood stabilizers are typically started when people have their first manic episode, or when they are experiencing a depressive episode and have a history of manic episodes. These medications help level a person's mood to a more steady state, which can help prevent future episodes.

How Do I Decide Whether to Use Antidepressant Medication?

If you've read this chapter so far, you know something about antidepressants and how they work. But this doesn't answer the question *Are they for me?* Imagine going to a therapist for an evaluation of your depression, and the therapist says, "I'd like you to consider taking an antidepressant medication." How do you decide what to do? How do people make this kind of decision?

Many people have fears about taking medication. For instance, people think taking medication is a sign of weakness. Erica worried that if she took antidepressants, it would mean she wasn't strong enough. She had always thought of herself as a happy person leading a stable, secure life. But her world came crashing down after a divorce. She attempted suicide. After this, she joined a women's support group and went back to work. Erica struggled for four years before she decided to see a therapist. At this point, she had many issues she wanted to work on. But Erica was surprised when her therapist talked to her about depression and suggested she might want to consider using antidepressants.

> *I hated the idea of medication. I really felt that taking meds meant that I had failed somehow, that if I were just strong enough, or just good enough, or just whatever enough, I wouldn't need drugs. It was certainly okay that other people needed meds; it didn't mean there was anything wrong with them, but it was not okay for me. To me, it meant that I was weak and disgusting. Even though I knew that thinking was flawed, I couldn't stop feeling that way. But I decided to go ahead and try the meds anyway.*

Erica was relieved when the medication she took helped her get better. But the decision to take antidepressants wasn't easy for her. She didn't know many people who were taking antidepressants—except her mother, which did not make her decision easier. She had seen her mother's depression as a sign of weakness and didn't want to see the same thing in herself.

All people have a time when they look in the mirror and see one of their parents. For most people, this can be disconcerting, no matter what characteristic is reflected back. But when people see a characteristic they don't like, it can be especially hard. If there has been something about their parents that troubles them, they may have sworn they'd never be like that. For instance, a person might have sworn, *I'll never yell at my kids like my dad yelled at me*, or, *I'm not going to worry constantly like my mom did*. The same phenomenon can happen with depression. If a person's parents were depressed, that person may have promised to be more positive, more active, more appreciative, and less dour and unhappy. This was similar to how Erica felt. Her mother had been depressed for many years, and Erica thought her mother lacked willpower and initiative—that she was mentally weak. Erica promised herself she would never be weak like her mother. Now her mother was finally taking antidepressants, and Erica herself was being confronted with a diagnosis of depression and a recommendation to take antidepressants.

Erica had to make a decision about her life. If she continued to see her mother as weak, she would probably reject the idea that she, herself, was depressed and needed medications. It would be too deflating to be in the same category. On the other hand, a diagnosis of depression might help Erica see her mother—and herself—with new eyes. Maybe her mother was doing the best she could with her depression. Perhaps it wasn't her mother's fault she was depressed. In turn, Erica might be able to see herself with some compassion.

Erica was able to choose to see both herself and her mother with new eyes. Over time, Erica was able to use this experience as another way to find her own identity. Yes, she realized, she had depression too; but this did not mean that she "was" her mother.

Brent also had trouble with the idea of taking medications. He had been in therapy for two years, and while his recovery from an eating disorder was going well, his depression wasn't improving.

> *My therapist recommended I try antidepressants. He could see that no matter how hard I was working, I wasn't getting over my depression. I didn't really like the idea, but I went to the psychiatrist he recommended. The psychiatrist did a twenty-minute interview and suggested imipramine. At first I did not get the prescription filled, thinking it was given too easily. How did the psychiatrist really know I needed medications? I carried the slip of paper with the prescription around with me and felt like I had a snake in my pocket. Weeks went by. But my depression got worse, and my therapist encouraged me to try the antidepressant. Finally I got the prescription filled, and it did help, though I had a lot of side effects . . . my mouth was dry, and I felt really sedated. The worst thing was decreased sexual ability. I went back to the psychiatrist, and he gave me a prescription for a different medication.*

When the psychiatrist gave me the prescription, I agonized over the idea of taking medications. Taking them just confirmed my diagnosis of depression, and I felt weak and ashamed about that. I knew that if the antidepressants did work, I'd feel guilty about needing them. But I did take them, because I was even more afraid of the depression.

Brent's experience raises an important point: there is generally no rush to take antidepressants. This can be a good route to follow if the depression is not life threatening or severe. You can take some time to learn some things about yourself and establish a trusting relationship with a therapist. Then, if you do decide with your therapist that medication might be helpful, you have already established good groundwork. And if the antidepressants help with the depression, you've got someone to help you celebrate the changes and build on the successes. Medication does not take the place of seeing a therapist, but it may be another useful way to treat your depression.

How long you wait before taking antidepressants is something that you and your therapist can discuss. It depends on the severity of the depression and the progress made without antidepressants. If the depression is not interfering greatly with everyday life, and you are making improvements, you may not need medications. If, on the other hand, depression is threatening your will to live, you may want to consider antidepressants right away.

Brent had tried for two years to overcome his depression without medication. Some might say he didn't need to wait this long. But there were two factors in operation here:

- He was working with a therapist and seeing some progress. He maintained hope that he could rise out of the depression fully. He needed the time to see that therapy alone was not going to alleviate his depression. But that does not mean at all that his two years in therapy were wasted. He had learned a lot in therapy that helped him in his struggle with depression. The medications were just another part of his treatment. And Brent took antidepressants for a relatively short period of time (about a year). They gave him the boost he needed, and he's been well for many years since without them.

- Brent was quite determined to overcome depression without medications. For many people, having control and a sense of mastery is important. There's nothing that says you "should" take medications. When the time came for Brent to consider medications, he had learned what he could and could not do on his own to reduce his depression.

Brent's story raises another important point. He was very thoughtful about his decision to take medications. He legitimately asked whether a psychiatrist who didn't know him well could determine his need for medications. Because there is no exact way to diagnose and treat depression—it doesn't show up on an x-ray—people may find it especially difficult and especially important to trust the psychiatrist who prescribes their medication. Although this was difficult for Brent, he did have some reasons to trust that taking antidepressants was the right decision. He trusted the therapist who referred him to the psychiatrist for antidepressants. After two years of working with him, Brent felt confident his therapist knew him well. He could also trust his own knowledge. He knew he was depressed and stuck. Even though he wasn't sure about the physician from just one meeting, he was able to accept the medication because he could trust his own knowledge and his relationship with his therapist.

What if you are in a situation where you do not have a therapist or anyone else to help you make this decision? Or what if you are just beginning to recognize your depression?

Here are some guidelines to use in making the decision about whether to try antidepressants as part of your treatment for depression.

1. Remember that taking medications is just one part of the work you'll need to do to overcome or live with depression. Some people get so focused on the medication question that it gets "bigger than life."

2. You need to have confidence in the physician you see. Feel free to ask as many questions as needed to gain that confidence.

3. Usually, there should be no rush to take antidepressants. If you don't believe that medication is the path for you, don't feel pressured into it— unless, of course, you realize that you're at a point in your depression where you need to let others make some decisions. Even if antidepressants are suggested and you choose not to take them, keep working with a therapist on your

depression. Together, you can decide at a later date if you need to revisit the question of medications.

4. Remember that many medications have side effects and risks (pages 167–169 and the appendix describes these). Some medications may have side effects that are intolerable to you. Some medications for depression or anxiety should not be used by recovering people. If you are recovering from addiction, take the physical consequences of your disease into consideration. Also, if you have a history of liver damage or seizures, be sure to tell your physician. Some medications will not be appropriate, or you will need a smaller dose.

What Is It Like to Take Antidepressant Medication?

You may wonder, *Will I stop being "me" if I take an antidepressant? Will it give me some sort of high? Will it just make me oblivious to my problems?*

The answer to all of these questions is no. Antidepressants do not change people or make them high or oblivious to their problems. In fact, many people who have taken antidepressants describe it as something that doesn't change their life directly. Rather, they say antidepressants provide a stable foundation so that they can make changes. Melvin Konner wrote an article for *The New York Times Magazine* about depression and antidepressants, using his own experience as a point of reference. He said, "For me the medicine became a platform on which I could function in a very different way."[5]

Tanya did not become a different person when she took antidepressants, but she was better able to cope with her problems. Like Brent, Tanya had been depressed for a long time and had been working with a therapist. When her therapist suggested taking medications, she thought a long time before deciding to try them. At the same time, she continued attending a support group and seeing her therapist. When asked if the medications made any difference, she said:

> *Yes. I saw things were a little better. I seemed to be more tolerant of others and less judgmental of myself, and I felt like I was making pretty good decisions. I could think so much better. I immediately started doing better in the college classes I was taking. But the most astounding thing was how the people in my life saw the improvement. Comments came from people who didn't even know I was on meds—my boss, for instance, although he still pushed my buttons and I still dreaded going to work every day. But there was a difference— sometimes I was actually able to let things roll off my back for real, not just pretend to. I don't mean to say that it was a huge difference, that everything was just rosy, but it was different. I could handle things better.*

Tanya seemed to become more resilient. As she admits herself, the problems didn't go away. She still had a job she didn't like; her boss was still insensitive; college was still demanding. But with the changes occurring within her, the problems affected her less. She could use her energy to continue her personal growth, rather than battle the world.

After a while, Tanya quit her job and started her own business. She said, with justifiable pride, "My ex-boss is currently my biggest client!" When people are depressed, they often stay in intolerable situations, mostly because they don't have the energy to make changes. Obtaining some relief from depression often creates a window of opportunity for people to let go of old ways of living and begin new, healthier ways. Tanya is able to look back now and say:

Through my passage of recovery from depression, I experience life on life's terms. I go through my ups and downs, but they are normal, everyday ups and downs, not exaggerated ups and downs. After being diagnosed with depression, getting therapy, and taking medication, I have an emotionally stable life that I never dreamed possible.

The path ahead of Tanya may not be easy. Managing her own business requires a great deal of self-discipline, which has been a problem for her in the past. She also misses the stimulation of taking college classes. Plus, she sometimes wonders if some of the symptoms of depression may be recurring. But Tanya is staying on the path. She's facing everyday problems of living and resolving them. She's also learning to recognize and deal with depression. She continues to see her therapist and go to her support group. Tanya has a good foundation for continuing her climb out of depression.

Taking antidepressants also gave Paul the stability he needed to deal with his problems. Paul had been depressed for so long that he thought his days free of depression were brief manic episodes. Life without depression was a new experience for him.

> *I experienced relief from the depression within four days of taking Prozac. I began experiencing what I had formerly labeled mania on a daily basis and now realize that it is life without depression. I found everyday tasks, such as cleaning my house and getting myself ready for work, easier. I started exercising, taking a good long walk almost every day. I haven't yet experienced the depression I had before. I occasionally experience some symptoms if I get overly tired or have a stretch of stressful days. Even when life gets hard, the Prozac helps keep me steady enough to deal with the problems. The problems in my life got a lot worse for a couple of years—but I didn't consider suicide. I went through some disastrous relationships with women; my daughter went through a difficult adolescence; I failed some important exams for work, lost my job, and incurred huge financial problems from being unemployed. But with Prozac, I didn't die.*

Being on medications did not transport Paul to a fairyland. Paul had a lot of problems to face—he had to learn how to develop healthy relationships with women, how to deal with his teenage daughter as she raged through adolescence, and how to go on when doors closed on his chosen career path. But the key fact was that he was able to walk through the depression and stay alive. He could do what he needed to do to stay on the path.

Now Paul has made some satisfying changes in his life. "A year ago I remarried and opened a business. I am happier now than I have ever been in my life." Paul saw his career problems as an opportunity and found new ways to use his talents. No doubt he will still bring some of his old issues to his new relationship, but he's learned what they are and can talk about them openly. He's not ashamed of who he is; instead, he's grateful for the support he's had and the wisdom he's gained.

Anthea found that taking antidepressants reduced the symptoms of her depression enough that she could take a fresh look at her problems. She had struggled with dysthymia and episodes of depression for years, and was reluctant to take any kind of medication. She was self-reliant and thought if she just worked hard enough at her depression, she could get through it. She first took Tofranil, one of the earlier tricyclics, and was somewhat disappointed with the results. It diminished her depression, but the side effects were so aggravating she couldn't enjoy the result. She went back to her doctor and was given a prescription for one of the newer antidepressants.

For me, it was just like taking aspirin. No side effects—and no jolt of good feelings. But something happened. Somehow, it lifted me over the void. The void, the abyss, was still there. But I didn't get sucked into it anymore. I could somehow—just somehow—let myself be carried

over it. I had a feeling I needed to come back to the
abyss someday, but it could wait until I was stronger.
For now, what I needed was just to get to the other side
of it. All my negative thoughts just weren't there. Bad
things, hard things, still happened, but I could deal with
them without tumbling into that black hole.

Anthea still had plenty of things to work on. Antidepressants didn't take that away. And it didn't take away her conviction that there were deep places within herself that she needed to explore. But during depression, the most important task is to stay alive and get through life's everyday dilemmas.

Raul battled dysthymia with occasional periods of fullblown depression. He was well educated, and because of his intelligence and likability, Raul often landed high-level, responsible positions. But every time he was able to put together a period of stability, it seemed to fall apart. His self-esteem was plummeting, and he began to seriously consider suicide. After realizing that he couldn't stop the slide by himself, he began seeing a therapist and started medications.

My personal opinion is that the medication saved my
life. I do not take it to get happy, but to get out of bed.

With all of these success stories, a person could get the idea that taking antidepressants works for everyone. Unfortunately, this isn't true. For many, success takes more than medication; it also takes months, or even years, of hard work in therapy and self-help groups. At one point,

Taylor hit a rough spot in her recovery. Reflecting on the role of medication in resolving her depression, she said:

Meds won't cure you by themselves. You are still responsible for your actions or lack of actions. And it's still difficult to do the things you need to do for yourself. I still need to go to meetings; I still need to work the Steps; I still need to call my friends and my sponsor. I know I haven't been doing those things, and I'm not doing too well as a result. Maybe meds can help, but just like anything else, it only works when you work it. (I hate it when God talks to me through my own mouth!)

Taylor could reflect on her situation with some humor. She took the medications, started to climb out of the hole of depression, and could see that there was hope for her life. But, as was pointed out in so many of the stories, she still had hard work ahead.

Some people get little or no relief from one antidepressant and may need to work with their physician over a period of time to find a different antidepressant, or a combination of medications, that helps. For others, the benefits don't outweigh the side effects. Still others simply feel no different on medications and decide that this route is not for them. Antidepressants are not magic pills. But as shown by the stories in this chapter, they give many people the foundation they need to cope with life's difficulties.

What Are the Side Effects of Antidepressant Medication?

Antidepressants, just like any other medication, have their downsides. Depending on the type of medication, side effects can range from inconvenient to life-threatening. Most of the time, and for most people, the side effects are minor compared to living with the depression. But it's important to know what the expected side effects are for any medication prescribed.

Common Side Effects

Side Effects	What to Do
Dry mouth	Drink lots of water, chew gum, suck on hard candy.
Constipation	Eat bran cereals, prunes, and other fruits and vegetables. Exercise.
Bladder problems (difficulty emptying bladder)	Call your physician if you experience pain or if this side effect is interfering with your daily life.
Sexual problems (increased or decreased interest in sex, or increase in time required to experience an orgasm; men may not be able to maintain erections; women may not have orgasms)	See your physician if these problems interfere with daily life.

Blurred vision	See a physician if this does not pass quickly. It can occur when you first begin antidepressants.
Dizziness when rising from a sitting or lying position	Rise more slowly when getting up from a chair or bed. Sit on the edge of a chair or bed for a moment before standing up. The dizziness, which is due to a quick drop in blood pressure when getting up from a chair or bed, is called *orthostatic hypotension*. If it continues and interferes with daily life, talk to your physician.
Drowsiness	Do not drive or operate heavy equipment if you feel groggy or sedated. This usually passes within two weeks.
Weight gain	Ask your physician if you can switch to a different medication.
Nausea or diarrhea	See your physician if this does not pass within two to three weeks.
Abdominal distress	Try taking antacids and antiflatulents. These can be bought without prescriptions.

Headaches	See your physician if this problem does not go away soon.
Nervousness/ agitation	See your physician if this does not stop during the first few weeks.
Sleep problems (insomnia or drowsiness)	See your physician if sleep patterns do not improve within a few weeks. Sleep is also affected by depression, so it's best to wait a few weeks after starting a new medication to see if sleep patterns improve.

Differing Responses to Side Effects

Everyone responds to antidepressants a little differently. Anthea's experience, mentioned earlier in this chapter, illustrates two extremes. She could not tolerate the side effects she had on Tofranil. Her depression was lifting, but the medication decreased her ability to be sexual. When her doctor switched her medication to a newer antidepressant, she experienced no side effects. On one medication, Anthea's side effects were significant; on another medication, they were absent. Some people are afraid to talk to their doctor about side effects, thinking they should be able to tolerate them. Anthea's story illustrates the importance of asking questions and speaking up when things don't seem right.

Other people have different experiences. Although antidepressants helped Bonnie, she wasn't sure in the beginning if the side effects were tolerable.

The side effects were mostly diarrhea—the first day was hell. But after about three days, everything went pretty much back to normal. My sex drive decreased at first. But after about four or five months, it seemed to come back, maybe not completely, but I'm thirty-eight years old, so I'm sliding down the wrong side of that "sexual peak" thing anyway.

Bonnie's libido, or sexual interest, may have started to return after four or five months because her depression was clearing. Her body may also may have been adjusting to the medication. Over time, she may want to review how the medication may be affecting her sex drive. Age does not necessarily mean a person experiences diminished interest in sexual activity. It's possible that a lower dose or a different medication may help Bonnie regain her full libido. She will decide if and when this is an important consideration for her.

It took some time for Arnette to find a combination of medications that worked for her. And in the process, she gained weight. The more typical side effect of the newer antidepressants is weight loss. But as Arnette's story points out, different people have different side effects. It's best to talk openly about them and come to terms with them.

I gained ten pounds a year for two years during the course of taking Tegretol, Pamelor, Depakote, and

Zoloft. I complained about it to my doctor, explaining
that taking medication for depression and gaining
weight from it can make a depressed person depressed!
He did say that taking the medication was a double-
edged sword. So what is one to do? Be happy and
fat . . . or depressed and skinny? Not much choice. The
medicine makes me crave sweets, which is unusual for
me. I don't usually like sugar.

Arnette decided to quit the medications altogether, and she lost weight. After two months, she was happy about her slim figure, but symptoms of severe depression started to return. Arnette recognized that the benefits of managing her depression far exceeded the disappointment of weight gain. She went back to her doctor and started a different combination of medications. She made sure she exercised, tried to eat healthy foods, and decided to live with any weight gain she might have. For most people, five pounds a year are not life-threatening. If weight gain or other side effects continue to be a problem for her, she could ask her physician to prescribe one of the newer antidepressants.

A person with an eating disorder may not be able to stay on track with weight changes so easily. In that case, a different medication, redoubled commitment to Overeaters Anonymous or another self-help group, and therapy for symptoms of bulimia, anorexia, or compulsive overeating may be needed.

Some people sleep more when they begin taking antidepressants, and some find their sleep disrupted. Jennifer found she had sleep problems when she first started taking Prozac:

I initially experienced some sleep interruption, but that passed within a few weeks. That was the only side effect I noticed.

Others notice that they dream more or have more vivid dreams. Increased dreaming may be due in part to the depression lifting and in part to the medication. But sleep problems, especially during the first few weeks of taking antidepressants, are not unusual. This seems to be more true for the SSRIs and the other newer antidepressants. The important fact to remember is that this side effect typically subsides with time.

Sometimes, though very infrequently, people taking antidepressants will find that their brain chemistry has been adjusted too far in the opposite direction, triggering a manic episode. When this happens, they become agitated, can't sleep, have a tremendous amount of energy, and feel euphoric. Some people have trouble discerning the difference between feeling normal and moving into a manic episode. If you experience any of these symptoms, it is important to contact your physician.

The side effects we have been discussing so far are relatively mild. Although quite rare, some severe reactions can also occur. Here is a list of considerations that anyone taking antidepressants should be aware of:

- The older types of medications, tricyclics and MAO inhibitors, can cause changes in blood pressure and heart rhythms.

- SSRIs and many of the newer antidepressants should never be taken within two weeks of taking the MAO inhibitors.
- Some antidepressants lower the seizure threshold. This means that someone prone to seizures, or with a history of them, may start to have seizures when antidepressant medication is taken.
- With all antidepressants, it is important that the liver and kidneys are functioning reasonably well in order to metabolize the medications.
- No long-term studies have been done to determine the overall effect of antidepressants on the body. People have stayed on antidepressants for years, and to date, no obvious problems have been seen. Still, no one knows for sure that long-term use will not have negative effects on the body.

Potential serious problems, along with the fact that the effects of long-term use are unknown, make it important to work closely with, and ask questions of, your doctor.

Combining alcohol and other drugs with some antidepressant medications can produce severe problems. With most antidepressants, use of alcohol and other drugs is strongly discouraged. In itself, alcohol is a depressant and not a logical beverage for someone who is struggling to overcome depression. Beyond that, the combination of alcohol and other drugs with antidepressants can be dangerous.

- When a person is on MAO inhibitors, wine and beer can cause a dramatic increase in blood pressure and, potentially, death.

- Tricyclics and MAO inhibitors enhance the effect of alcohol and other drugs. This means that they interact with alcohol and drugs and magnify their effect in unpredictable ways.

The SSRIs and newer antidepressants do not seem to interact with alcohol and other drugs in the same way that other antidepressants do. However, in most cases, no use of alcohol is advised.

When and How Do I Stop Taking Antidepressant Medication?

After taking antidepressants for a while, a person will want to know, *When should I stop taking them?* There seem to be two main paths that people follow with antidepressants. Some people need them for a relatively short period of time, a year or less; others find they need to remain on them indefinitely. And some people who take antidepressants for a short time return to them later in life if depression recurs. Let's take a look at short-term and long-term use.

Short-Term Use of Antidepressants

Some people take antidepressants for a short time, six to twelve months, and are able to get back on track. It takes about two months for most antidepressants to fully take effect and stabilize in a person's body. Then it can take another period of time, at least four more months, for the person to incorporate all the changes that come with being less depressed. A person needs time to learn to live without depression and to be able to sustain that state confidently before discontinuing medication.

People who can benefit from short-term antidepressant therapy are often those who are experiencing a major depression for the first time or have most of the symptoms of a major depression—difficulties with sleeping, eating, anxiety, concentration, and low mood. The trigger is most likely to be external or social—job loss or breakup of a relationship. Depression is quite alien to these people. They are not used to being depressed; it is not their usual state of mind.

Dr. Bert Pepper, a noted psychiatrist, has found that about half of the patients that he sees strictly for medication monitoring (in contrast to psychotherapy) needed medication for less than six months.[6] These patients continued seeing their psychotherapists, but a relatively brief course of medications got them through a period when they were stuck in depression. Dr. Pepper sees the six-month medication period broken down in this way: two months are needed to get stable, and an additional four months are needed to incorporate behavioral changes and make adjustments.

Beth's depression came suddenly after a series of setbacks in her career. Once a vibrant, active, outgoing woman, she lost all confidence and self-esteem, became withdrawn, barely ate, and was having difficulty sleeping. When she was near suicide, she went to a psychiatrist, certain that she was in a hole so deep she'd never get out.

*I took Paxil for about eight months. My psychiatrist
assured me that my depression could be turned around
and that I could be "jump started" within a few months
on the medication. I was very skeptical. Now, four
months without Paxil, I feel as fine and stable and
serene as I did while on it. I have read a great deal
about that family of drugs [SSRIs], and I am convinced that taking [Paxil] was the correct thing to do.*

After she was stabilized on antidepressants, Beth got
back on a regular program of exercise, her relationship
with her partner improved, and she regained her confidence. Beth needed antidepressants for only a short
time.

Mike looked back and realized that he'd experienced
depression pretty regularly during the winter. (This type of
depression is known as *seasonal affective disorder*.) He had
learned to live with this, almost to expect it. But he wasn't
prepared for what happened to him when his marriage
broke down. His self-esteem crashed and he couldn't think
well or make decisions. He wasn't sleeping or eating, and
he seriously considered suicide. This depression went on
for months, longer and more severe than any he had experienced before. Finally, he saw a psychologist and started
individual therapy to work on some important issues sur-
rounding his divorce, and he was referred to a psychiatrist
for medications. The physician recommended Zoloft, which
he took for about nine months.

*The first thing I noticed was that I was able to concen-
trate. This started within the first week of taking medi-*

cation. As the weeks went on, I felt my self-esteem improving. Now I'm much more optimistic about life—about my life. I still get the seasonal blues, but even that isn't as bad and I recognize it for what it is. (I mostly get slowed down and sleep a lot.) But the sense of worthlessness and hopelessness is gone. And I don't think about suicide. I'm not sure how it happened, but Zoloft almost seems to have triggered a permanent change in my brain chemistry. Or maybe it just gave me my first glimpse of a normal, healthy, positive outlook on life and its possibilities.

Mike, too, got a "jump start" out of his depression. He still had things to work on—for example, he knew he was still feeling grief about his divorce and needed to look at what part he might have played in it—but now he could do that with clear eyes.

While many people need to take antidepressants for only a few months, it's important not to quit prematurely. Some people quit taking their medications just when they begin to feel better, thinking they don't need them anymore. But if they quit before they have really made the needed adjustments, they may sink back into depression.

Barry had been depressed off and on for years, and he was in the midst of a custody battle for his three children. He had also lost his job. He wasn't sleeping or eating well, and his fatigue and inability to concentrate only added to his feelings of worthlessness. He did start to see a social worker for therapy and then a psychiatrist for medications, but he stopped both when his depression started to lift. The depression got unbearable again, and he went back to therapy and medication. Soon, this became a pattern. He said tearfully:

I don't really like to continue taking medication and seeing a therapist because I want to get on with my life. I don't really believe in all this stuff anyway. I'm the type that always thought people who said they were depressed were just copping out. Besides, I'm afraid the judge will hold it against me if he sees I'm in therapy and on medication. I might not get custody of my kids.

Barry has some difficult choices to make. Clearly, he feels so much shame about his depression that it is difficult for him to accept help. He may also have reasonable fears about how decisions are sometimes made about child custody. But without treatment for depression, Barry was going to stay stuck in a very bleak place. He knew that if he stayed depressed, he wasn't going to be able to take care of his kids even if he did obtain custody of them. And without being able to work, he couldn't support them. Neither option was good. Ultimately, Barry decided to renew his efforts with therapy and medication, and to stay committed to that path. It's difficult to know how long Barry will need to stay on medication, but if he can put together four to twelve months of solid time on it, he may then be able to try tapering off. With the help of his doctor, he can monitor his depression and decide when to stop taking medication.

Jack also had second thoughts about continuing his medication. He didn't want to take it in the first place, and after about nine months, he decided he was better and didn't refill his prescription.

I didn't give it much thought. I just knew that it cost a lot and that I didn't like taking it. It wasn't that I had any side effects—I didn't. It was because taking it kept reminding me that I had a psychiatric illness.

After about two months of being off medication, Jack could feel himself slipping into depression again. He talked to his therapist, and they both agreed it would be better if he got back on the antidepressant. He also continued his self-help program and therapy sessions, and was able to discontinue his medication with the support of his therapist after just six more months. Several years have passed, and though life has thrown him many challenges, Jack has not needed medication again.

Long-Term Use of Antidepressants

Because few long-term research studies have been done with antidepressants, not much is known about the way long-term use affects the body. It's possible that negative side effects will show up. Therefore, most physicians plan for their patients to stop using antidepressants at some point. However, some people find that they are at such high risk for recurring depression that going off medications is intolerable. For many of these people, it is not just a matter of having a better life; it is a matter of having a life worth living.

People with long histories of depression, with recurrent depression, or who are older when they have their first episode may be at greater risk for another depressive episode. John Greden, a psychiatrist, uses the following rule of thumb when trying to determine whether a person is likely to have another onset of depression. He says that (a) if people experience depression for the first time at age fifty or older; (b) if they have had at least two episodes after the age of forty; or (c) if they have had at least three episodes at any time in their lives, they are likely to experience depression again.[7] Still, this isn't true for everyone. Some people fit in one of these categories but will never experience another bout of depression.

Remember that these findings about who is at high risk for relapse to depression are generalizations: they may or may not apply to you. If you fit the criteria, you won't necessarily experience depression again, but it is something to consider. If you are at high risk, you may want to continue with antidepressants and make sure you are taking other action to help stave off depression. The good news is that even if you are at high risk for repeated depression, effective treatment is available.

Long-term use of medication is also necessary for people with bipolar disorder. They generally need to stay on mood stabilizers for their lifetimes. Over time, they may be able to work with a physician to find a different dose, or combination of medications, that will lessen any side effects. But because of the nature of this disease, the likelihood of a recurrent manic or depressive episode is high. Just as people in recovery from addiction need to keep going to Twelve Step meetings, people with bipolar illness need to stay on lithium (or other similar-acting medication). Even if life seems to be going very well, maintaining the program and the prescription keeps relapses from recurring.

Discontinuing Antidepressants

The best time to stop taking medications is when depression has let up and life is relatively stable. Even when a person is feeling well, discontinuing antidepressants during a time of turmoil may be asking too much for a brain and body to handle.

Frank was a very competent young man who had to drop out of college and return home to his parents when his depression hit. He was devastated, but he started taking antidepressants and worked hard with his therapist to get back on track. Within six months, he felt like his old self again and was ready to return to school. To give himself a fresh start, he chose a different school. At the same time, he decided to stop taking his medications. He didn't tell anyone because he thought it wouldn't matter. After all, he felt better, and he was embarrassed about being on antidepressants. He didn't want to risk the stigma of anyone finding out about his depression at his new school. But the combination of attending a new school, moving in to a new place, and making new friends created enough stress to throw him off balance. Fortunately, Frank took quick action. He found a new therapist, got back on antidepressants, and started doing well again. There's a good chance that Frank will be able to stop taking his antidepressants soon, now that both he and his life are stable again. But this time, he's not in any hurry about stopping them and wants to plan the change with his doctor.

There is an increasing number of reports of a withdrawal, or "discontinuation," syndrome associated with SSRIs. A variety of uncomfortable symptoms may appear for days or weeks after a person stops taking these medications. It is very important to understand that the symptoms may be related to withdrawal. Some people (and physicians) mistakenly believe that emergence of these symptoms indicates a returning depression. A wide variety of symptoms may occur, but the core discontinuation symptoms are the following:[8]

- fatigue
- chills
- headaches
- digestive problems such as diarrhea, nausea, or vomiting
- insomnia
- difficulty concentrating
- agitation
- dizziness
- odd sensations such as tingling or "electric shocks" in parts of the body
- tremor
- muscle pain
- dyscoordination (clumsiness)

These symptoms can start to occur within one to four days of discontinuing the medication and have been reported to last three days to thirteen weeks. It's important to know that they can begin even after only one dose is missed. Paxil has been associated with most of the reports of withdrawal symptoms. Reports of withdrawal symptoms have also been published for Prozac, Luvox, and Zoloft.[9] The symptoms don't seem to be related to the medication, dose, or length of time a person is on the medication. It may take a little longer for the withdrawal symptoms to show up for Prozac and Zoloft, as these have longer half-lives; that is, they last longer in the body. Discontinuation symptoms may also appear with newer antidepressants when enough time has elapsed for people to have had experience with the medications. The older antidepressants, tricyclics and MAO inhibitors, also have withdrawal symptoms associated with them, though these have never received much attention.

The best method to use in discontinuing antidepressant medication is a long, slow taper, over at least one to two weeks, in partnership with a physician. At the end of the taper, you may be taking a very small amount every other day. While vague symptoms may continue to appear, it's important to let the healing power of time take its course. This is also the time to make sure you are working with a therapist to consolidate your gains and stay on track with the improvements you've made.

What's in the Future for Antidepressants?

Herbal remedies, such as St. John's Wort *(Hypericum per-foratum)*, are gaining more visibility and interest. While anecdotally, many people have found relief from their depression by taking St. John's Wort, there have not been enough studies completed to test its safety and effectiveness. There have been some recent studies in Germany, however, which show that the herbal remedy shows some promise. The National Institute of Mental Health is taking the herbal remedy seriously and has funded a major study at Duke University to test its effectiveness as an antidepressant.[10] It is known that St. John's Wort should never be taken along with other antidepressants, as serotonin levels may be extremely affected, even causing a fatal reaction.[11]

Another dietary supplement, known as SAM-e (S-adenosylmethionine), shows promise as an antidepressant. It is currently available in other countries by prescription[12] and may act by increasing the number of neurotransmitters in the brain.[13] However, an insufficient number of studies have been done to determine whether this is an effective antidepressant.[14]

New medications for depression are being created nearly every day. Most undergo testing in other countries before being approved in the United States by the Food and Drug Administration. In the search for a better antidepressant, scientists are looking for improvement in three areas: faster time of onset, fewer side effects, and lower cost.[15] A "perfect" antidepressant, as envisioned by pharmaceutical researchers, would involve all these three areas as well. In addition, the price would need to be low enough so that managed care companies would approve it for their formularies, or individuals could afford to pay for it out of pocket.

What If I Am Recovering from Addiction?

If you're in recovery from addiction, it's especially important to seek help for depression for two reasons. First, the combination of depression and addiction is not uncommon, and professionals do know how to help. Second, letting the depression continue can make you more vulnerable to relapse to alcohol or drug use. Treating the depression can also help your recovery from addiction.

Some people in recovery from addiction have an erroneous belief that they should never use medications such as antidepressants. They often worry about two things. First, many people believe that Alcoholics Anonymous is against taking antidepressants because recovery from addiction and taking antidepressant medication won't work together. This is not true. In fact, antidepressants may be an important and necessary part of addiction recovery. Alcoholics Anonymous is not against antidepressants or other necessary medication prescribed by physicians and used as directed. In fact, in a pamphlet called *The A.A. Member—Medications and Other Drugs* AA members are encouraged to use medications such as antidepressants as necessary: "A.A. members and many of their physicians have described situations in which depressed patients have been told by A.A.s to throw away the pills, only to have depression return with all its difficulties, sometimes resulting in suicide. . . . It becomes clear that just as it is wrong to enable or support any alcoholic to become readdicted to any drug, it's equally wrong to deprive any alcoholic of medication which can alleviate or control other disabling physical and/or emotional problems."[16]

Second, people in addiction recovery often worry that antidepressants may be addictive or may trigger their addiction to alcohol. This is not true either: antidepressants are not addictive.

In this section, we will look first at stories of people who worried that taking antidepressant medication and recovering from addiction wouldn't work together. Then we will look more closely at the erroneous belief that antidepressants are addictive. Finally, we will examine what is known about the effects of medication on addiction.

Medications and Alcoholics Anonymous: Can the Combination Work?

It's common for people in addiction recovery to worry about combining medication with the program of Alcoholics Anonymous. Sylvia, who has been in recovery for six years, worried about whether she could attend Alcoholics Anonymous and take antidepressants. However, she was glad she decided she could:

> Don't listen to that inner voice that says you're a failure if you use meds. You just have to realize that when there's something wrong and there's a way to fix it, your responsibility is to fix it. Sometimes you need a little help.

Terri also decided to take antidepressants several years after she had been in recovery. Looking back, she realized she'd been an addict since the age of sixteen and depressed since she was even younger. Her adolescence was stormy, with both addiction and depression raging within her. She finally got into addiction recovery in her late twenties, but life just didn't seem to come together for her.

I was totally drug-free for seven years. But I can't describe the depression I was in. It was totally debilitating. I can see now that it affected everything I did, all my thoughts, all my decisions. Finally I decided to get help. I still can't believe I didn't drink, drug, or kill myself. Within two weeks of being on Zoloft, for the first time in my entire life, I knew what it was like to get out of bed and face a day like a normal person. If you suffer from depression and addiction, make sure you are not self-medicating on alcohol or drugs, and get to a doctor who can help you. Depression is not your fault.

Terri fought hard for her recovery, both from addiction and depression. Because the illnesses started so early in her life, she didn't know that what she was going through wasn't the way life had to be. She was ready to accept the responsibility of being an adult and maintaining her sobriety. Terri thought that if she "white knuckled" it and tried to "grow up," she would overcome her depression. Medications helped Terri start living a life she didn't know was possible.

Some people in Twelve Step programs are fine with the idea of antidepressants; others are adamantly against it. Again, Alcoholics Anonymous, as a general organization, is not against the use of antidepressants.

Depression is not new among Alcoholics Anonymous members. In fact, the first historians who read the letters and writings of Alcoholics Anonymous's beginnings found signs of depression among members then, in the late 1940s and 1950s. Early members understood the pain and turmoil of depression and its potential impact on sobriety. Bill Wilson, the cofounder of Alcoholics Anonymous, suffered from depression for about eleven years, between 1945 and 1955.[17] In the book 'Pass It On,' Marty M. said: "It was awful. There were long periods of time when he couldn't get out of bed. He just stayed in bed, and Lois [his wife] would see that he ate. An awful lot of people believed he was drinking. That was one of the worst rumors we had within A.A."[18] Bill's lifelong secretary, Nell Wing, said: "He would come down to the office many times and sit across from me and just put his head in his hands and really not be able to communicate, just almost weep. He used to talk about it. It baffled him."[19] She also said, "It always puzzled him, why he had to endure this suffering since, as he often said, he was so fortunate and had so much to live and be grateful for. He felt sure it must be biochemical."[20]

Bill Wilson sought help from general physicians and psychiatrists. But at that time effective treatment, either in the form of psychotherapy or medications, wasn't available. He spent time in psychoanalysis with Dr. Harry Tiebout; he went to an osteopath and cut down on sugar; he undertook a program of walking and breathing; he worked his Twelve Step program harder; he tried vitamins such as B-12 and niacin, and hormones; he even tried LSD, as a new drug of the day. Unfortunately, Bill Wilson was not able to find a treatment that could relieve his depression.

Today, much more is known about depression, and many people in Twelve Step groups recognize that they have both depression and alcoholism. Here is what several people have said about how using medication and Twelve Step groups together work for them.

Chris was active in her community's Alcoholics Anonymous group, but wasn't sure how to handle the topic of taking medication.

At first I felt very guilty about taking the medication because it went against what I was being told by some people in the program. I have talked about taking the medication at meetings since then. I wanted people to know that if a doctor diagnosed them manic-depressive, they should take the medication for their recovery, not against their recovery. I have had a couple of people walk out. This was very sad for me because then I felt that I had to hide this. For my recovery, I don't.

Gregg continued to attend Alcoholics Anonymous meetings despite the repercussions he experienced and the stigma he felt from some people in his groups when he talked about being on antidepressants. He kept in contact with his sponsor and kept applying the Twelve Step philosophy in his daily life. After a while, he said:

People in the program are beginning to be more tolerant of people with mental disorders. That's because more people are coming in the program with it. These things all help; things are changing in the program.

Most of Amy's recovery work has been in Alcoholics Anonymous (AA), Overeaters Anonymous (OA), and

Adult Children of Alcoholics (ACA). In her AA group, no one talked about depression and antidepressants. Many of her friends in OA acknowledged taking antidepressants, but it usually wasn't talked about in any detail. However, Amy found many people in her ACA group, her "safe haven," whom she felt comfortable talking to about her decision to use antidepressants and with whom she could compare stories.

How comfortable people are talking about depression and antidepressants may vary among Twelve Step groups. Amy was fortunate because she was involved in several different groups and could find the support she needed for her depression in at least one of them. All over the country, different Twelve Step groups will be more or less comfortable accepting people who are on antidepressants, depending on the region, the group members, and their shared history.

Sylvia expected her Alcoholics Anonymous group to disapprove of her use of medications. But she didn't stay away from her meetings. Instead, she discovered that the group included people she could share her story with.

> I was surprised that I found as much encouragement at AA meetings as I did. I expected the opposite because I'd heard "no drugs whatever, for any reason" over and over again. I never believed that anyway. Even Bill W. said, "We are not doctors." I mostly know what drugs I can take, and when a doctor prescribes something for me that I don't think I should have (codeine cough syrup, for instance), I know to say thanks, but no thanks. But if I need surgery, I'll take

the morphine. I don't believe that God wants us to be in pain when there is an alternative. God just wants us to use our alternatives wisely. And as my sponsor said, "If you had a broken leg, would you refuse the cast?"

The main message is *Don't stop going to meetings.* Taking medication does not disqualify you from being a member in good standing! You may find more support and understanding than you expect. If you don't find the support you want, keep talking to your sponsor and continue to look for others in the Twelve Step program who share your story. They are there. You are not alone.

Medications and Addiction: Do Antidepressants Cause or Contribute to Addiction?

People in addiction recovery often worry that antidepressant medications are addictive. They don't want to be struggling to overcome one addiction just to replace it with another. But antidepressants are not addictive. As explained earlier in this chapter, antidepressants are not uppers. They do not make you happy or cheerful. A physician once pointed out that the best way to tell if a medication produces a high is to ask how much it is selling for on the street. Antidepressants clearly do not have a street market.

Many doctors use the analogy of diabetes to help people worry less about taking an antidepressant medication. The diabetic's pancreas does not produce enough insulin. An improper balance of insulin results in serious problems, including blindness, kidney failure, and loss of circulation. Although depression is not understood as well as diabetes, the same model works. For some reason, it seems that people who are depressed may not be able to maintain a balance of certain chemicals in the brain. Antidepressants help the brain to regain its natural chemical balance.

LaVon was considering taking antidepressant medication, but she became afraid when her mother said she "loved" Zoloft. Using Zoloft, her mother had found freedom from a lifetime of depression. But LaVon was afraid it might be addictive. She explained how her doctor helped her see the difference between addictive and nonaddictive chemicals:

> When my mom said she loved Zoloft, it was a red flag in my mind. Although my mother has never suffered from alcohol or drug addiction, I have, and I didn't want to put myself in a position where I "loved" any kind of pills. When I mentioned this to the doctor, he asked me if I had felt good when I had used drugs in the past. I said I felt powerful, competent, and self-confident, but never "good." He pointed out that people didn't get high on antidepressants; it was just a way to overcome a chemical imbalance in your brain.

Many people who are recovering from addiction are uncomfortable with the idea of taking any kind of medication, addictive or nonaddictive. They have struggled, or may still be struggling, with adopting the mind-set that life can be lived without chemicals. Even when they know that antidepressants are not addictive, they may have two feelings at the same time: one feeling is very logical, as they tell themselves, *This antidepressant is not addicting; it's a necessary and helpful medication*, and the other feeling is intense confusion.

The story of Henry shows how one recovering person decided to try medications. Henry had eight years of sobriety, was married and raising a family, and had gone back to graduate school. In spite of all his outward successes, a deep depression had tugged at Henry for as long as he could remember. Eventually, all his efforts started to unravel. His wife wanted a divorce. He couldn't find any common ground with other students at school. He felt utterly alone and had nowhere to turn for help.

> *I found myself crying frequently. I felt constantly desperate. My feeling of self-worth was gone—I was focused on my worthlessness. I felt suicidal. On Christmas Day I decided to drink first, die later. On my way to the grocery store to buy a bottle, I saw a friend from AA driving down the street. I realized that he was going to a local holiday marathon meeting. I turned my car around and followed him. When I arrived at the meeting, I told him how he had saved my life. He recommended I see a doctor in AA who is a certified addictionologist. The doctor was my family doctor when I was small, and I felt comfortable with him. I saw him the next day. He took a lengthy history and told me I had been depressed for some time.*
>
> *I don't believe I would have taken the medication if the doctor had not been in recovery. I never completely*

accepted the belief some people in AA hold—that a
person in recovery should never take antidepressants.
But I was afraid to lose my sobriety. I had seen people
in the grips of withdrawal from prescription tranquil-
izers and wanted none of it. The doctor won my trust.
He told me what to expect as possible side effects. He
helped me understand that it was medication for an-
other illness, using the insulin/diabetes model. He told
me not to stop taking the antidepressant on my own,
and he suggested that after I was less depressed and
my life had settled down, we would decide together
when I should stop.

On the face of it, Henry's story seems like an amazing and unlikely turn of events. He was desperate, and the help he needed came in the form of an Alcoholics Anonymous friend at just the right time and place. Even more remarkable, he had the name of a physician who not only was in recovery himself and a specialist in addiction, but who was his trusted childhood family doctor. You might reasonably ask, *How could this chain of events ever be duplicated in my life?* It seems remarkably coincidental. The exact same events, in that order, will probably never happen again. But other remarkable events will occur. People recovering from addiction have many stories that seem miraculous. Somehow, when people have been on a journey of openness and self-discovery long enough, they become more able to experience help or see help in all sorts of ways they wouldn't expect. What is there to learn from Henry's story?

First, keep going to meetings. All the years that Henry went to his Alcoholics Anonymous meetings, sponsored people, and used the Twelve Step philosophy in his daily life made a difference. Many times he might have doubted that this was enough. But because he stayed on that path and kept opening himself up to change and growth, he was at the perfect time and place when he needed help. In the most fundamental way, this is spirituality at work. Whether or not you believe in God or have a relationship with a Higher Power, you can prepare yourself for this kind of remarkable coincidence.

Second, look for a physician who understands recovery from both addiction and depression.

- Henry's physician was an addictionologist. After they get their medical degree, physicians can receive a certification in addiction by completing a special course of study and passing an exam. Addictionologists understand that addiction is a disease; they also understand how to support people in their recovery. While it would be wonderful if this training was mandatory in medical school, it usually isn't. Still, more physicians are getting training in addictions. Be sure to ask your doctor about his or her experience and understanding of addiction.

- The physician was recovering. For Henry this was especially important. It was a signal to him that the doctor would understand his concerns about taking any medication. Your physician may not be in recovery or may not make that known to you. But by asking questions about your doctor's knowledge and experience, you can decide whether you are comfortable or whether you prefer to consult with someone else.

- The physician was a longtime, trusted physician. In this era of health care reform, we may be often asked to switch doctors when our health care plan changes. Or we go to a clinic where we see the next doctor with an open appointment time. This makes establishing a relationship difficult. But Henry's experience points to the helpfulness of seeing the same physician over the long term. If you have a physician you trust, he or she might give you the assurance and direction you need about medications. However, it would have been better still if Henry's doctor was a psychiatrist. Psychiatrists have years of advanced education in emotional disorders and medications. (You may wish to refer back to chapter 5, pages 112–115, where we looked more closely at how to choose a therapist or physician.)

- Finally, the physician spent a lot of time with Henry. He did a lengthy history. He asked questions and described what medications do and what their side effects are. He also made a commitment to work with Henry until his depression improved and he was ready to go off medications.

The Effect of Medications on Alcoholism/Addiction

As pointed out several times in this chapter, antidepressant medications are not addictive. But exactly how do antidepressants affect addiction? The question really has three parts:

- Do antidepressants put you on a slippery slope toward reactivating addiction to drugs or alcohol?
- Does resolving depression increase the chance of staying sober?
- Do the same chemicals that reduce depression also reduce alcohol or drug cravings and therefore intake?

While the answers to each of these questions has been touched on earlier in the book, we will review them here.

First, do antidepressants put you on a slippery slope toward reactivating addiction to drugs or alcohol?

No research studies have found that use of antidepressant medication triggers a person's addiction. Nor are there any reports of this happening from psychiatrists or psychologists who treat addicts or alcoholics. Recovering people say that they see their two disorders as quite separate—they have an addiction and they have depression. LaVon's addiction was to "crank," an amphetamine-like drug or upper. She worried that taking antidepressants would start her down that path again. Instead, she found that antidepressants affected only her depression:

*Taking medications didn't affect my addiction—I was
five and one-half years sober when I started meds, so
my recovery had a life of its own. I haven't had cravings in a long time, and so far haven't relapsed.*

LaVon's addiction was stabilized with her Alcoholics
Anonymous program, and the use of antidepressants
didn't alter that. She was concerned about taking care of
her depression. LaVon was afraid that if she became depressed again, she would isolate herself, which in turn
would increase the chances of relapse to crank.

*Second, does resolving depression increase the chance of stay-
ing sober?*

What is the relationship between depression and relapse to
drug or alcohol use? On the one hand, the two are probably
so closely connected that research cannot easily untangle
them. Some people know instinctively that becoming depressed is a trigger for relapse. Many of the symptoms of
depression are exactly the same as the warning signs of an
impending relapse. What used to be called a *dry drunk*—
the negative state of mind often accompanying addiction
that some people can't get out of, even though they are
sober—may well be what we know today as depression. For
example, many people in Twelve Step recovery are familiar
with the acronym H.A.L.T., the reminder that if they get
too hungry, angry, lonely, or tired, they may be setting
themselves up for a relapse. The last three of those—
irritability, loneliness, and fatigue—are symptoms of depression too. A person who is depressed cannot simply

decide to not be angry, lonely, or tired. These may be warning signs that depression is returning.

Matt recognized this and decided that the best way for him to stay on track with both depression and addiction was to think of them as two separate diseases.

I have to be compassionate with myself and keep in mind that I have two problems. Abstinence is critical, number one. I know that if I drink or use drugs, I can't do the work I need to do to stay not-depressed. Drinking or using drugs would keep me down. Plus, I know my therapist couldn't help me with depression if I were using. It just wouldn't work. I accept the fact that I have two diseases, and it's not my fault. Even though the depression and the alcoholism happened simultaneously, they are separate. If I fix one, the other won't automatically go away.

Many of the same methods that help keep depression at bay fit well with reducing addiction relapses.

Third, do the same chemicals that reduce depression also reduce alcohol or drug cravings and therefore intake?

It's possible that some of the same chemical pathways in the brain are involved in both depression and addiction. Medications that balance a person's serotonin levels might correct the chemical problems that cause a person to become depressed and to use alcohol and drugs. Researchers hope that someday the neurotransmitter similarities between depression and alcoholism will be understood well enough so both can be treated with one medication. Prozac and other antidepressants are among those that are being studied for this purpose. So far, the results show some promise on a research level but less on a real-life level. For instance, there is research in which mice or monkeys are given free access to alcohol. When injected with Prozac, they drink less alcohol. Although what is true for monkeys in laboratory settings often turns out to be true for human beings, Prozac doesn't seem to make much of a difference in most people's use of alcohol. Some studies report that alcoholics on Prozac drink less at a time, or less per day, but do not necessarily achieve full abstinence.[21]

So far we have talked about whether taking antidepressants is a good idea for people who are in addiction recovery. Clearly many people benefit from their use. But if you are recovering from addiction and taking antidepressants, there are some special precautions you should know about.

Special Considerations for People Who Are in Addiction Recovery and Taking Medications

Some medications for depression or anxiety should not be used by recovering people. Some may pose risks that are intolerable to you.

If your body has been damaged by addiction, you may have to be more careful about taking antidepressants. People in addiction recovery may have liver damage or a history of seizures. Tell your physician about your health history. Some medications will not be appropriate, or smaller doses will be needed with certain medical conditions.

In general, monoamine oxidase inhibitors (the category of antidepressants described in detail at the beginning of this chapter) are generally not prescribed for addicts because of their low margin of safety. Certain foods are dangerous when taking MAOIs, and people who take them must be very conscientious about strict dietary restrictions.

Finally, if you are recovering from addiction, you may be in the habit of not following directions for drug use. Sometimes recovering people recognize their tendency from their using days to think, *If one works, two will be better!* This is dangerous thinking when taking antidepressants. Be sure to follow the directions for taking your antidepressants. Antidepressants are complex chemicals and need to be taken as prescribed.

What Does This Mean for Me?

If your therapist or someone else is suggesting that you consider taking antidepressants, keep in mind that you are in the driver's seat. Using antidepressants is not something that is done *to* you; it is something that you choose to *use* as one way to tackle your depression. It's important to be a smart consumer; you need to know (as much as possible) what to expect. You also need to be able to ask a lot of questions and to take your time in making such an important decision.

If you do decide to use antidepressant medication, feel free to ask questions of your physician. Here is a list of questions about taking antidepressants that people frequently ask. (The first five questions come from the United States Department of Health and Human Services.)[22] Your physician will probably give you this information. But this list may still be a handy review of the things you want to know as you begin taking any antidepressant.

1. When and how often do I take this medication?
2. What are the side effects of this medication?
3. Are there any foods I should not eat while taking this medication?
4. Can I take any other medication while I am taking this medication?
5. What do I do if I forget to take my medication?
6. How long will I have to take this medication?
7. What are the chances of getting better with this medication?
8. How will I know if this medication is working or not working?
9. What is the cost of this medication?
10. How can I, as a recovering person, be certain this medication is not mood-altering?

After you have started taking medications, you may find you have many more questions. For instance, you may not be sure if a change you are experiencing is associated with the medication. Or you may wonder if the medication is working at all. It's important to work closely with your doctor and to ask any questions that are on your mind. Dr. Dorothy Hatsukami, a psychologist at the University of Minnesota, said:

The thing I'd like most people using antidepressants to know is, if it's not working, or if you're having a lot of side effects, tell your doctor. I see too many people who tell me they just stopped taking their medications, or conversely, are miserable taking them. They might not realize that something can be changed—needs to be changed! It might not be the right dose or the right antidepressant.

Medications work differently for different individuals. You need to feel comfortable working in partnership with your physician to get the best combination of medication and dose.

The United States Department of Health and Human Services has five recommendations for people who are starting antidepressant medications.[23] This may be a helpful list for you to keep in mind.

1. *Keep all your appointments.* At first, your psychiatrist will ask to meet with you frequently to see how the medication is working and whether you are experiencing any side effects. After four to eight weeks, if you begin to feel better, you will probably have appointments once a month or two. If you stay on antidepressants for a long period of time, you may just check in once every three months. The assumption is that you are seeing a therapist regularly and more frequently to work on problems that may underlie the depression.

2. *Ask questions.* Every medication is different. Don't assume that just because someone is a physician they can know exactly how an anti-depressant medication will affect you as a unique individual. In fact, most physicians will count on you to tell them about your experience on the medication so they can make correct adjustments.

3. *Take your antidepressant as your psychiatrist tells you.* Antidepressants are complex chemicals and need to be taken as prescribed. Doses that are too high or inappropriate combinations of anti-depressants can make you sick or, in rare cases, even kill you, so it is important not to change the dose or use a friend's prescription. It's also important to keep taking the medication even if you start feeling better. You should only stop taking antidepressants according to your doctor's directions.

4. *Tell your psychiatrist about any side effects you're having.* Usually, these are most noticeable during the first few weeks of taking a medication. But if you are experiencing any side effects that have you worried, don't just assume that's the way it has to be. Call you doctor and describe what you are feeling. Changes can be made if needed.

5. *Tell your psychiatrist how the antidepressant is working.* If it isn't working, and four to six weeks have elapsed, you may need a different dose or a different medication.

Further Questions

I'm in recovery and cannot take mood-altering chemicals. Since antidepressants reduce or stop depression, aren't they considered to be mood-altering?

No, antidepressants are not considered to be mood-altering. If you take a mood-altering chemical, like alcohol or cocaine, you notice a change in your mood right away. Drugs that are categorized as mood-altering have fairly rapid action, with direct effect on mood. Antidepressants do not produce any discernible change in mood in the minutes or hours after they are taken. It is only over time (days, weeks, and months) that many people taking antidepressants will notice an improvement in their depression. Antidepressants help stabilize a person's mood so the person can begin making changes and improvements in life. Keep in mind that antidepressants do more than affect mood; they also improve sleep, appetite, and other symptoms of depression.

Why is it okay to consider using a prescribed antidepressant when it is not okay to use other drugs that change how people feel?

Drugs that people might use on their own to alter their mood are probably addictive. For example, some people try to improve their mood by taking alcohol, cocaine, or marijuana. Initially, these might seem to work. If people are shy at a party, they may find that a drink or two makes them feel bold. Or a hit of marijuana takes the dreariness out of a dull reality. But over time, tolerance develops, and they use more and more of the chemical, trying to recapture the effects. In the meantime, preoccupation with the chemical takes on a life of its own. Alcoholism or addiction results.

Prescribed antidepressants are created to be nonaddictive. People take them under the guidance of a physician and often receive psychotherapy at the same time.

I've been stable on meds for a period of time, but now they don't seem to be working like they used to. Could I be getting depressed again on medications?

Some people do find that a satisfactory dose loses its effectiveness over time. This does not happen to everyone. Little research has been done on this phenomenon, so it is not well understood. But psychiatrists are familiar with it and have methods of addressing it. Here are some of the most common options.

～

Your physician might prescribe a higher dose.
The following two stories show how this can work. Sarah belonged to a support group and started taking medications for her depression.

"I began at 50 mg of Zoloft . . . then a letdown . . . then went up to 100 mg and the same thing. Now I'm taking 150 mg and I've felt fine for a year and a half. Some other women in my depression support group stayed at the lower dosage and felt okay with it even after the letdown."

Howard had a good response to medication initially but later found that he, too, needed to have the dose reevaluated.

"I started off at 50 mg a day, which helped for about three months. Then I started feeling the same old feelings. I would be irritable . . . no one liked me . . . I was worthless . . . cluttered thoughts . . . obsessed with pessimistic thoughts . . . overreacting. My doctor upped my dose to 100 mg a day. I'm okay again."

You might be asked to switch to a different medication. This happens especially for people who need to be on medications for a long period of time. Over time, some people become very well attuned to their depression and their response to the medications they have received. George is truly a self-expert and needs to be because he has had so much experience with recurring depression over the course of his life. Here is his perspective.

"It's very important to know as quickly as possible when my depression is returning, because this usually means discontinuing whatever I'm taking and going to another medication for a while. Someday I hope I can find something that will work long term. With new medications being developed all the time, I think that's possible."

A small dose of another antidepressant medication might be used in addition to the one you are taking. In the 1960s and 1970s, when antidepressants were new, the accepted practice was to prescribe only one antidepressant at a time. Now it is accepted practice in some situations to use a secondary antidepressant to help the effectiveness of the main antidepressant.[24] Thirty percent of depressed people will not be helped by a particular antidepressant. Rather than give up, a physician may prescribe a small dose of another medication to use in addition to the original one. But not all types of antidepressants can be combined. It takes a skilled practitioner to know which types of antidepressants, and dosages, are safe to use together. In some cases, you may need to go off a medication for a period of time before going on a new one.

~

What if I can't get stabilized on the highest recommended dosage?

Don't be discouraged and don't give up! Keep going back to your physician with information about what is happening to you. There is a good chance you will find relief by changing to a different medication or a new combination of medications. Feel free to go to another physician or ask for a second opinion. There are new developments every day. And keep going to therapy and attending support groups.

What medications are most likely to be used as an adjunct to an antidepressant?

It depends on the problem. If you are taking a selective serotonin re-uptake inhibitor (SSRI) such as Zoloft, Paxil, or Prozac, and it doesn't seem to be working as effectively as it could, your doctor may prescribe a small dose of desipramine or another type of tricyclic. Or your doctor may prescribe Synthroid, a thyroid hormone that improves the effect of SSRIs.[25] If you are experiencing anxiety, your physician may prescribe desipramine in addition to, or instead of, your usual antidepressant. If you are experiencing insomnia, you may be prescribed Desyrel.[26] However, don't be too quick to think that you need another medication until you have gotten fully stable on your original medication. Sometimes symptoms such as anxiety or insomnia may increase initially when you go on an antidepressant.

I am depressed and have an eating disorder; my doctor says that Prozac will help both. Is that true?

In April 1994, the Food and Drug Administration approved the use of Prozac for bulimia. The president of Anorexia Nervosa and Related Eating Disorders, Juean Rubel, is quoted as saying, "It isn't a magic bullet, but for the people for whom it works it's tremendous."[27] Some people with bulimia say that Prozac evens out their appetite so they do not feel such an intense need to eat large quantities of food at one sitting.

I am taking an antidepressant and I'm having insomnia; I can't fall asleep, or once I do fall asleep, I can't stay asleep.

Some medications, like Desyrel (trazodone), may be prescribed for sleep. It has a very mild antidepressant effect, which might not be enough for most people as their sole antidepressant. But its sedative effect is significant and helpful for many who are taking other antidepressants.

Should I take Xanax for my sleep problems?

No, there are two reasons why Xanax should not be taken for sleep problems. First and most important, Xanax belongs to a class of medications that is addictive, especially for chemically dependent people. Second, its powers of inducing sleep wear off over time. Then a rebound effect can occur, whereby a person has even more difficulty with sleep.

I am taking an antidepressant, and I'm having problems that are sexually related.

Some people notice a loss or decrease in sexual drive on antidepressants. For men, this may be particularly noticeable, since the loss in sexual drive may show up as impotence or delayed orgasm. In some cases, this can be a significant problem, especially if the man is in a relationship where the couple is trying to get pregnant. For women, a decrease in sexual drive may show up as difficulty in reaching orgasm or reduced sexual desire. Women may not report this difficulty, since they can still participate in sexual intercourse. Whether you are a man or a woman, if the antidepressant you are using is interfering with your ability to enjoy sexual experiences, talk to your physician.

Some people notice an increase in sex drive while taking SSRIs. This could simply be a return to normal for them if they had a decreased sex drive during their depression.

I am taking an antidepressant, and I want to get pregnant. Is this okay?

In most cases, your physician will recommend discontinuing antidepressants at least during the pregnancy and perhaps through the period of time you breastfeed your child. However, research is being done in this area, and on occasion some antidepressants may be allowed. As this is an important, changing area, you will do best to talk to your physician about your options.

I am an elderly person. Can I use antidepressants?

Your physician will probably prescribe a lower dose than is recommended for younger people. Older adults' metabolism is generally slower, so lower doses produce the same effect. Standard adult doses in older people may produce greater side effects. However, the required dose is quite variable, so it is important to work with a knowledgeable physician. Good results with antidepressants for older people have been reported.

I am stable on medications, but I have a tough time during my premenstrual phase. Is this normal? Can it be helped?

Talk to your psychiatrist about varying the dose to follow your monthly cycles. Some women find that they feel better during the premenstrual phase with antidepressants. For example, Cindy, in her thirties, reported:

> *I'm taking 50 mg a day of Zoloft. My PMS isn't as bad as it used to be. I'm not crying or angry or feeling like I hate my husband . . . yet.*

What Can I Do to Help Myself?

1. Has a mental health professional suggested that you begin taking antidepressants? If you are considering antidepressants, what questions do you have? Make a list of your concerns. Who could you trust to answer these questions? Could you make an appointment with a psychiatrist to go over your list? You may want to get a second opinion for some questions, for example, "Given my medical history, is this the best medication for me?" Gathering thorough, factual information may help you decide whether or not antidepressants would be helpful and safe for you.

2. If you are taking antidepressants, are you using them as prescribed? Do they seem to be working well for you? If they are not working, they might not be the right antidepressant for you. Talk to the person who prescribed your antidepressant for recommendations.

3. If you are taking antidepressants, are you also doing other things to help your depression? Many people find that therapy and other methods of self-exploration and behavior change can contribute significantly to recovery from depression; they can even help prevent future episodes.

Chapter 8

Depression and the Family

On my worst days, the best thing that people could do for me is give me the knowledge they are there . . . and then leave me alone. It was hard, but through my depression I learned, on the simplest level, how important my children and family are to me.

➤ Lee, who has suffered from depression
and anxiety for twenty years

Psychotherapy and medication are the most important tools to use in healing from depression. But family and friends can also play a useful and important role in helping people who are experiencing this illness. Peter Kramer, author of *Listening to Prozac,* concludes his book by acknowledging his family and stating, "The drug will never be invented that sustains the spirit the way a family can."[1]

When you're depressed, you might become frustrated and want people to leave you alone. Yet isolating yourself can damage your relationships with friends and family. At some point, it may even seem that the relationships are not worth salvaging. But you can work through your depression without losing all your relationships. When you are out of your depression, you'll be glad you did what you could to keep relationships with family and friends intact.

The Importance of Family

What Family and Friends Can Do for You

If you are depressed, your family and friends can have a tremendous effect on how you feel. You may feel annoyed with them, very dependent on them, grateful to them, or some other feeling entirely. But it is important to remember that your illness—depression—does affect them in many ways. Of course you didn't ask to be depressed. Still, your family and friends notice that you are not yourself and they react in a variety of ways. Some will drift away. Some will flutter about you and try to give you advice. Others will not speak of their concerns because they feel awkward and confused. They don't understand what is happening to you. Some of these responses may feel helpful, some annoying. Or what feels helpful one day may feel annoying another day.

If you feel burdened by the responses of your family and friends, remember that you are not responsible for their reactions to your depression. You can be sensitive to their pain or uneasiness, but you can't change their reactions. The best you can do is to focus on your own recovery from depression. Dan could see the family dynamics around him quite clearly, even though he was in the middle of his depression.

*The big danger I notice in my own family is that I can
let my feelings of helplessness drive me away from
being myself, or I can start expecting the impossible of
myself. The truth is, my dad has helped me through
this much more than my mom. My mom is so worried
about doing or saying the wrong thing that I feel like
I'm walking on eggshells around her. My dad doesn't
do or say much, other than that he loves me and he's
there for me. That's a support that's helped me more
than he'll ever know.*

Dan showed a tremendous amount of compassion and
understanding about both his mother and his father. While
he recognized that his father's reaction is most helpful, he
understood that his mother is who she is and that he
doesn't need to change her or react to her.

Families can also help you as you struggle with your depression. Liz didn't believe in therapy. She was unhappy,
but since everyone in her family was dysfunctional, she
didn't think she had much chance of being happy anyway.
She figured she would just have to get through life the best
she could. But watching how her sister coped with the illness helped Liz learn how to get help for her depression.

*My sister offered to take me to a therapist, but I said
"no way." I refused for a year and a half as I watched
her get better. It was her example of mental healing
that convinced me I could get well too. I remember feeling much like Dorothy asking the Wizard, "Is there
something in your bag for me?"*

Sometimes families cannot help, but friends can. Their help may come in small or large ways. Noah recalled how his co-workers helped when he was depressed.

Sometimes at work I just couldn't hold it together any-more, and I'd go into an empty conference room and cry. I will forever be grateful to my co-workers who took time to sit with me. They didn't try to tell me what I should or shouldn't do. They didn't spread it around the office that I was having crying spells. They knew I was depressed, getting help in the best way I could, and that I wasn't going to just "cheer up." I knew they cared.

The most important thing Noah's friends did may have been simply to sit with him. They didn't try to fix him or talk him out of his depression. William Styron, distinguished American author of several novels, had a friend who took on a more active role.

By the time I had commenced my autumnal plunge my friend had recovered (largely due to lithium but also to psychotherapy in the aftermath), and we were in touch by telephone nearly every day. His support was untir-ing and priceless. It was he who kept admonishing me that suicide was "unacceptable" (he had been intensely suicidal). . . . I still look back on his concern with im-mense gratitude. The help he gave me, he later said, had been a continuing therapy for him, thus demon-strating that, if nothing else, the disease engenders last-ing fellowship.[2]

Styron needed the active help his friend gave him. And in the process of giving it, his friend continued in his own recovery from depression.

What You Can Do If Someone You Know Is Depressed

How can you help someone who is depressed? The answer is somewhat paradoxical: on the one hand, it is important to do what you can to help the person get help. On the other hand, it's important to keep in mind that you cannot cure another person's depression, even with the best intentions and information. You might feel helpless, frustrated, scared, and confused. It's important for you to stay on an even keel and live your own life as best you can.

Here are some practical things that can help you if a family member or friend is struggling with depression:

- *DO listen.* You don't need to solve the person's problem or take it on as your own. Just listening is enough.

- *STAY connected.* The person who's depressed may be isolated, may not initiate contact, or may refuse invitations. You can still do things to stay connected without expecting the person to reciprocate or reconnect with you. For example, you can send an occasional card saying "thinking of you" and update them on what's new with you, or you can extend an invitation to get-togethers or events to which you'd normally include him or her. In doing so, it's best to be upbeat and matter-of-fact, just as you might be with someone who has a broken leg or other disability. For example, you might say, "If you're up for it, some of us are going to a movie and we'd love to have you join us." It's not a good idea to attach pressure, point of view, or advice. Avoid adding statements like, "Are you sure you won't come? It's just for a little while. You might feel better if you got out." If you're met with refusal, you can say something like, "Okay, maybe next time. Would you like me to pick something up for you when I'm out?" or, "Okay, I'll give you a call tomorrow."

- *SUGGEST that the person get help.* One framework for doing this is the "four I's"—"I see, I feel, I want, I will." Here is how you can use it:

  "I see *you're different than you usually are (name what you see; for example, you've been so withdrawn lately, so sad . . .).*"

  "I feel *concerned about you.*"

  "I want *you to get through this hard time.*"

  "I will *help you get the help you need.*" *It's helpful if you get a couple of names and phone numbers of resources ahead of time that you can give the person. Or, you could offer to accompany the person to meet with someone who may know what to do.*

  Shame, stigma, or the magnitude of depression itself may prevent the person from taking you up on your offer. You might need to approach your friend or family member more than once over a period of time. Do not gauge your success only on whether you personally succeed in getting a person to a therapist.

- *Take ACTION if the person talks about suicide or behaves in a way that leads you to wonder if she or he is considering it.* Asking a person about suicide will not "give them the idea" or make the situation worse.

- CONSIDER *seeing a therapist yourself or finding a support group if your loved one struggles with depression, and it is affecting your life.* You may not be able to change his or her life, but you may be able to continue on with yours. Your getting help may influence the other person to seek help too (though this should not be the goal).

- *AVOID the temptation to try to fix the person.* Suggestions about what worked for you or someone else or other intimations that the solution is easy "if only they would . . ." may make the person feel like more of a failure and less willing to maintain a connection with you. Chances are the depressed person is perfectly intelligent and would have acted on simple, rational solutions if she or he could.

- CONVEY *hope, faith, love, and courage.* Let the person know that while he or she may not be able to see a way out of the depression, you can, and that you appreciate the courage it takes to hang in there.

Doing any or all of these things may not bring the person out of the depression. It's hard to watch someone you love, who you know could be a vibrant, happy person, remain caught in the throes of depression. You may see the person make progress, gain a foothold, then slip back again. The most important thing to remember is that people *do* get well and that recovery from depression is possible. It may take time, but during that time, you can make sure that your life is going forward and that you're welcoming your loved one along too.

What Does This Mean for Me?

Some friends and family members may be able to support you when you are going through depression, while others may not. Some people may react to you in ways that feel intrusive—trying too hard and being overly attentive. Or they may become angry and try to control you. How they react to your depression depends partly on them and *their* way of dealing with difficult situations. It may also depend on you and how you interpret their reactions and their attempts to help you. It's okay to tell them how you feel about their response to you and your depression. They may or may not be able to change. But keep the door open to them as much as you can. Know that even if their concern feels off the mark now, it may be what will sustain you later. Keep looking for friends and others who will understand you. Reaching out to people who can help you is an important part of healing from depression.

Further Questions

My family is trying to fix me; how can I get them to back off?

You might be feeling a little irritated by your family's efforts to help. It's natural for family members to want to help, and it's a symptom of depression to want your family to leave you alone. First, make sure you are getting help from someone—that you have at least made an appointment with a psychotherapist or psychiatrist. If you are trying to tough it out alone, your family may be giving you an important message: there is help available, and it would be best to reach out and get it. Second, it's okay to tell family members that while you appreciate their concern, it doesn't feel helpful to you at this time. Perhaps you would like people not to ask you about your depression so often or not to give you advice. Maybe you can come to some agreement about what would feel better. Still, people are who they are and they may continue to show their concern in ways that don't feel helpful. Try not to shut yourself off from all your connections with them.

Why are my friends ignoring me?

Your friends might be ignoring you for two reasons:

- First, they might feel helpless when they are around you. They can see that you're down and not doing well, but they don't know what to do about it. Feeling helpless can be scary for some people, so they may ignore you to avoid their own feelings of fear or helplessness.

- Second, you might (without even realizing it) have given them signals that you don't want them around. When people are depressed, they shut down emotionally and socially. In your depression, chances are you haven't been calling them or inviting them to do things. Your friends may not understand that your lack of attention toward them is due to your depression. Could you tell them that you are depressed and are not intentionally rejecting them? This might not instantly change their behavior, but it may increase the chance that they will find some ways to be with you more.

What Can I Do to Help Myself?

1. Take a look at how your family and friends are reacting to your depression. Can you see that they may be reacting out of their own fear or misunderstanding? Are some people more comfortable with you and your depression?

2. If family and friends are not being helpful, is there a way that you can tell them what you need? They may not be able to respond as you would like, but by letting your own thoughts be known, you will have made it possible for change to occur. And you will have moved from a position of helplessness to one of some power. In depression, this can be important.

Chapter 9

Depression as a Spiritual Phenomenon

Leaving behind nights of terror and fear
I rise
Into a daybreak that's wondrously clear
I rise

⌁ Maya Angelou

Most of what people hear and read about depression implies that it is wrong, that it's bad and must be fixed—as if depression were a foreign invader, an enemy to be eliminated at all costs. Of course this illness is painful; it's not something most people would choose to experience. But there is another side to depression. For all its pain, depression can bring messages that can help people improve their lives—messages about the way they want to live, about their values, about what matters most to them.

As a society, we do not talk much about depression except in the context of new drug developments. But there are expressions of it in poetry, literature, and music—a noble, redeeming side, the side that prompts people to think deeply about life. In the depths of depression—no matter what the cause—people confront some of the most important questions that are ever asked, questions of ultimate value and purpose. Seeking the answers to these questions can help people heal from depression or avoid its recurrence.

In this way, depression can bring spiritual gifts. The word *spiritual* is used here to mean the deepest parts of ourselves. People often emerge from depression having learned things that enrich their lives.

Nurturing the spirit helps to maintain emotional balance. However, please remember as you read this chapter that it is not a substitute for getting treatment. Many people need treatment from a mental health professional to overcome depression. All of the information you have read in earlier chapters still applies: depression is a disorder that can and should be treated.

Asking Spiritual Questions

There are problems that physicians and therapists cannot solve. This leaves people with essentially spiritual questions, the kind of questions that have many answers. And only the person asking can decide which answers fit best. For instance, people with heart disease, cancer, or AIDS must ask themselves how to best live their lives in the face of persistent illness. Depression can also be a chronic condition. Some people will need to spend a good part of their lives struggling with mild depression (dysthymia), recurrent depression, or long episodes of depression. How can they best live their lives when they aren't seeing the results of their hard work toward recovery from depression? This is a question science cannot answer.

For many people, depression is relatively mild and short-lived, amenable to treatment without recurrences. But as people struggle with depression, they also find themselves asking spiritual questions. As Judy struggled with her depression, she found herself asking such questions. Even though she seemed to have an exciting career and many friends, Judy felt numb, cut off from her feelings, and disconnected. In the depths of her depression, she said:

I have found that the deciding factor in choosing to live or die, when it comes down to that final question— and I can only speak for myself—is hope. Sometimes a glimmer is all that is needed. But sometimes even that glimmer is hard to find. If there is no hope, there is no reason for me to live.

Judy had to work hard to find reason for hope. It wasn't a question her therapist or physician could answer for her. *Is there hope?* is a spiritual question, and Judy had to answer it for herself. But during the process of struggling with the question, she learned how to cope with her depression.

Asking questions about the meaning of life is often referred to as a spiritual quest or a spiritual journey. St. John of the Cross wrote about the process of the spiritual journey.[1] In his treatise, he discusses "the dark night of the soul," which he describes as the bleakness of losing contact with a Higher Power. He sees this as a normal stage in the progression toward spiritual wholeness. At first, people working toward spiritual growth are filled with a sense of wholeness and fulfillment (or in his terms, closeness to God), but later they enter a period where they feel as if they have lost it all. (This sometimes happens with people working a Twelve Step program. They may come to a comfortable relationship with a Higher Power, but over time—perhaps even months or years—they feel as if they have lost the connection that sustained them in the past.) St. John of the Cross believed that walking through this night brought a person to a new and deeper relationship with God.

It is common in spiritual journeys to go through dark periods, usually after periods of progress. Being at the low point in the cycle, or dark period, can mean that your spiritual journey has taken you to a place where you are ready to face hard issues, ready to face new questions and truths. You may repeat this cycle several times.

Recognizing When a Spiritual Journey Alone Cannot Help Depression

When people are in the bleak, despairing part of the cycle, they may be confused about its meanings. They may wonder if there is any point to the despair, if they are just depressed. This confusion is described in a book called *The Feminine Face of God.*

> *If we have learned to trust the inner self when it sings, can we trust it when the singing goes flat or stops altogether? What is it that we trust anyway? By the time we get around to asking that question, all the beautiful*

*and inspiring words we've read or heard or even spo-
ken ourselves seem at best distant echoes of something
we once believed. At this point, as one woman put it,
"We want to know whether we're going through a
'dark night of the soul' or a depression. If it's a 'dark
night,' we'll try to get through it. If not, we want
Elavil."*[2]

The fact is, people may need both antidepressants *and* a
helping hand through the dark night. As noble as a spiritual
quest might be, it cannot occur when people are stuck in
the depths of a major depressive episode. People need to be
standing on more solid ground in order to struggle with the
big questions of life. Being in psychotherapy or on antidepressant medication does not stop spiritual growth.
Rather, treatment can provide the solid ground that is
needed to proceed with spiritual growth. It's often only
when people are safely past the darkest days that they can
take a step back and look at what can be learned from
depression.

Some people seeking spiritual growth are reluctant or
ashamed to get help for depression. They think that if they
were more spiritual, meditated more deeply or longer,
prayed more sincerely or more often, they wouldn't be depressed. This thinking contains several fallacies.

First, depression can be an independent disorder that
comes of its own accord. Yes, paying attention to spiritual
aspects of life may help prevent or lessen it. Nevertheless,
the disorder, like any other illness, strikes people regardless
of the quality of their spiritual lives. This may seem clearer
if you compare it to having an illness such as alcoholism or

cancer. It doesn't make sense to think, *If I were a better person, I wouldn't be alcoholic,* or, *If I prayed more, I wouldn't have gotten cancer.* Nor does it make sense to think, *If I were further along on my spiritual journey, I wouldn't have gotten this depression, or, at least I'd be able to get over it.* Human beings are vulnerable to various diseases. The goodness of one's soul cannot give blanket immunity. In fact, when people believe that they should be "above" getting depressed, they actually set themselves apart from the human race by establishing unrealistic expectations for themselves. As pointed out in chapter 2, depression can strike anyone.

Second, depression may be a sign of progress in a spiritual journey, rather than failure. For some people, it means that they are ready to face hard issues and feelings, perhaps ones they have been skirting for years. Until now, they may have been able to grow into competent, stable, mature adults. But further growth might not be possible until these issues are faced. Some people have buried deep grief over profound losses. Others have covered up years of abuse. Now, in their stable adulthood, they have accumulated enough inward strength—and perhaps a relationship with a Higher Power—to turn around and stare into the eyes of long-hidden ghosts.

Third, sometimes people look back on their lives and can see ways that depression had been present for years, but just under the surface. Novelist William Styron experienced depression later in life and reflected:

> [A]fter I returned to health and was able to reflect on the past in the light of my ordeal, I began to see clearly

*how depression had clung close to the outer edges of my
life for many years. . . . In re-reading, for the first time
in years, sequences from my novels—passages where
my heroines have lurched down pathways toward
doom—I was stunned to perceive how accurately I
had created the landscape of depression in the minds
of these young women, describing with what could only
be instinct, out of a subconscious already roiled by dis-
turbances of mood, the psychic imbalance that led
them to destruction. Thus depression, when it finally
came to me, was in fact no stranger, not even a visitor
totally unannounced; it had been tapping at my door
for decades.*[3]

In some mysterious way, Styron was prepared for his depression. No one who has been through depression would
ever will it again. But many people can see in retrospect
how its presence made sense in their lives.

When to Get Help

How can you decide whether you are experiencing a major
depression or simply a rough spot in your spiritual journey? You can use these five signs to differentiate between a
spiritual crisis and a major depression:

1. You identify with many of the symptoms of
    major depression outlined in chapter 1, such as
    apathy, appetite problems, sleep problems, fa-
    tigue, lack of energy, feelings of worthlessness
    and hopelessness, trouble concentrating, and
    recurrent thoughts of suicide.

2. You are not moving forward. You tend to your usual spiritual practices—meditation, prayer, readings, or working with a spiritual director—but you still feel stuck.

3. You have no hope.

4. You are aware, even dimly, of old grief, trauma, or losses from the past, but have not resolved or come to a comfortable place with them.

5. You have attempted or are seriously thinking of committing suicide.

If you are experiencing any of these five signs, professional help will help you deal with your depression so that you can safely continue your spiritual journey. Assuming that you are willing and able to seek professional help for the depression as needed, let's look at the ways a spiritual perspective can help during this time.

Recognizing the Role of Depression

Knowing that depression can carry lessons in its wake, that it can be a path to something new, may make it easier to bear. You may even wish to ask yourself, *Does my depression have some necessary role to play?* Depression often plays a significant role in changing people's lives.

Some Spiritual Images of Depression

Here are two images of depression that sometimes give people hope as they travel through its dark waters.

As a Bridge, Not an Abyss

The way you've always lived your life suddenly isn't working anymore. But you don't know how to change it, how to make things better. While you are in the midst of depression, it feels as if the misery will last forever. There seem to be no openings, no bright spots. If you can imagine this dark period of time as a bridge instead of an end point, you might feel less despair. A woman, Rose Huntley, wrote about her experience:

> When it seems that the foundations have been ripped out, those of us who experience the void feel lonely, desperate, raw, vulnerable, exposed. We may feel abandoned and a bit frantic. The old reasons do not work any more, and we cannot make them work. A friend . . . once said, "We experience the liminal place as a void, but through the power of faith we can interpret it as a bridge." This spoke to my experience.[4]

It is telling that she uses the word *liminal*, which means "threshold." Author Joseph Campbell, who studied common themes in myths, uses the same idea:

> The familiar life horizon has been outgrown: the old concepts, ideals, and emotional patterns no longer fit; the time for the passing of a threshold is at hand.[5]

Viewing depression as a bridge, or as a threshold to another room, can require a great deal of imagination. You might feel as if depression is a deep, bottomless hole or a black wall that you can't get around. But if you can imagine it as a bridge, you can begin to see that depression is not the end. Even when you imagine depression as a bridge, it might seem like a very long, covered bridge. You may know intuitively that your experience with depression will change your life, but you don't know what lies ahead. One of the main characteristics of depression is hopelessness about the future. So it takes courage and faith to believe that something worthwhile lies beyond the depression, even if you cannot see it or imagine it. Depression can be a bridge, a place of transition. It is not a place where you will be stuck forever.

As Transformation in the Forge

A forge, defined as a furnace or hearth where metals are heated or wrought, can also represent depression. In Celtic religion, sacred spaces were spaces where transformation occurred, like the fiery forge or a mother's womb. The human void of suffering is also a sacred space: there is uncertainty, waiting, vulnerability, and pain. Like all transforming experiences, it is a mystery. Why do we need to experience it? What will come out of it? Theologian Shawn Madigan said:

> The Celts sensed that forces of good spirits and bad spirits vied for power in transforming space. These vulnerable spaces bore the mystery of the impenetration of the human and the holy. Only a burning power of hope can transform the terror of the void into the promise of new life.[6]

During depression, it can feel as if everything is dead within you. But there is work under construction. Profound internal changes are occurring. While it is sometimes impossible to be outwardly productive during depression, the psyche is continuing to move and evolve within.

As people work with depression, as they quit resisting and allow it to occur, they may discover new truths about their lives and themselves. They may also make space for new truths by letting go of things within them that have already died. Often people try to define who they are or determine their worth by external measures such as power and possessions, and they are left not knowing who they really are inside. They are left with a feeling of emptiness. If they can stop trying to fill the emptiness inside themselves with busyness or material possessions, they may begin to find new ways of being fulfilled. Thomas Moore, who wrote a special section on depression in his book about the soul, says, "Melancholy thoughts carve out an interior space where wisdom can take up residence."[7] Maybe human beings need to go through phases of emptiness and pain in order to see life and themselves in new and more complete ways.

Some Spiritual Messages of Depression

Depression can indeed help people learn more about their lives. Here are some of the messages that depression may bring:

You May Need to Change Your Direction, Your Values

Depression sometimes brings the simple message that people need to change their lives. Such changes may be internal, external, or both. Often when something goes wrong, people assume that something outside needs to be changed. Instead, people may need to accept who they really are. Consider the cartoon that shows a duck standing on a psychoanalyst's couch: the psychoanalyst says, "I'm sorry, I can't help you. You *are* a duck." Who we are at the core is unchangeable. And sometimes it can take a long time to recognize, accept, and love that core self.

Once people have come to know and accept themselves, they may find that some external changes are necessary. For although the core self is unchangeable, the expression of that self in the world is changeable. In other words, people may need to make changes in the way they live so their lives better fit who they are.

After experiencing depression for almost a year, Bob started to realize he needed to make changes in his life. He had been taking antidepressant medication and had begun to feel better, but still he saw no reason for joy. Here's how he talked about his life:

> *In my thirties, I decided it was time to settle down. I got a job in a software business. It wasn't really my area of interest, but it paid well. I met a woman who wanted to get married, biological clock stuff. She wanted kids, and so did I. So we got married—for the wrong reasons, I'll admit; we never really did love each other. So now here I am, forty years old. I've lost my job and my wife is filing for divorce.*

Bob found the key to his recovery from depression when he began to see his depression as a signal that something in his life needed to change. He didn't need to simply feel better about his situation. He needed to change it or at least allow the changes to occur. While he could improve his ability to function with medications, his depression was likely to recur unless he altered something in his life. He could cling to the belief that his job and his partner were right for him, or he could let go of that image. He could change his life to reflect who he really was by acknowledging that he was now free of a job he didn't like and a partner he had never loved. Letting go of what once seemed to fit is one of the hardest things that people are called to do in life.

People have choices as they come out of depression. They can try to patch together the remains of the life they had before, or they can make bold changes and create a whole new life. Some people even come out of depression with renewed vigor and commitment that provides them with a new understanding of life.

You Are Deeply Connected to the Human Race

Many truths of life seem paradoxical. For example, people who are depressed may come to understand that being absorbed in grief is an utterly lonely experience, but that it is an experience that most human beings share. Again, while people who are depressed usually feel very much alone, they may become aware of just how difficult life is for all human beings. In this way, they become aware of the bonds they share with others. For instance, you may go to the bakery counter to pick up a weekend treat, feel pleased to see a familiar woman waiting on you, and think, *She is in her forties, always there with a smile when I stop in. How can she care so much about her job? What gets her out of bed? No doubt by this time in her life she has experienced failure, been rejected, had hopes dashed, and lost people she loved. Yet somehow, she continues.* And so do you. While the reasons for each person's suffering may be unique, the fact that he or she suffers is not.

Looking back on his depression, Jim realized that there were others who understood his despair and that he needed to reach out to them.

> *I knew I needed lots of help. But I wondered,* Who can I trust? *I decided it was those who left me feeling the safest.*

You cannot overcome depression alone. You need to reach out for help. And when you reach out, you may realize that suffering is a characteristic that connects you with other human beings.

The Moment at Hand Is the Most Important

One of the great spiritual principles is to live in the moment. It is the basis of the spiritual practice of meditation. In meditation, people devote energy to focusing on the present. Becoming aware of the value of living in the present is important to healing from depression. People who are depressed typically hold a negative view of the past, present, and future: *In the past I was a failure, now I am nothing, and the future holds no hope.* In fact, depression is often accidentally reinforced by taking the bleakness of today and hurling it into tomorrow. To counter this, people with depression are advised to focus just on today. The simple slogan "One day at a time" is a good reminder. And if the task at hand seems overwhelming, they need to break it down into the smallest pieces they can handle.

A Painful Childhood Can Be a Source of Strength

The depression and despair people feel as adults can stem from childhood trauma or other difficulties. When people revisit the vulnerability or devastation they experienced as children, they can become filled with despair. But the fact that they survived loss and pain as children can mean that they have special strengths that they might not otherwise have; for example, they may have learned to be especially resilient or especially sensitive to people and situations around them. While people would never ask for a painful childhood, living through such a childhood can bring gifts that help in adulthood.

Courage Matters

Depression is often described as a black cloud. As mentioned earlier, people who are depressed are generally filled with despair. Human despair, whether clinical depression or not, exists and needs to be recognized and tended to. Those who experience despair and struggle through it are courageous.

An elderly woman recalled a turning point during a particularly difficult time in her life:

That night I thought long and not without despair
about what must become of me. I wanted very much

to be a person of value and I had to ask myself how this
could be possible if there were not something like a soul
or like a spirit that is in the life of a person and which
could endure any misfortune or disfigurement and yet
be no less for it. If one were to be a person of value that
value could not be a condition subject to the hazards of
fortune. It had to be a quality that could not change. No
matter what. Long before morning I knew that what I
was seeking to discover was a thing I'd always known.
That all courage was a form of constancy. That it was
always himself that the coward abandoned first. After
this all other betrayals came easily.[8]

In the course of depression, people gain new truths about who they are. It takes courage to reclaim themselves. Depression brings the message that courage counts.

As people reach the other side of depression, they often realize that they have gained a new perspective on life. When they can step back, they realize that they see life differently, that they have grown. Renowned African American novelist and anthropologist Zora Neale Hurston wrote:

Well that is the way things stand up to now. I can look
back and see sharp shadows, high lights, and smudgy
in-betweens. I have been in Sorrow's kitchen and
licked out all the pots. Then I have stood on the peaky
mountain wrapped in rainbows, with a harp and
sword in my hands.[9]

During depression, life can seem flat and meaningless. But after depression, people look back on their lives and see how their depression affected much of what they do and who they have become. While they felt as though they were drowning, they may actually have been climbing to a new peak.

What If I Am Recovering from Addiction?

The Twelve Step Philosophy

The Twelve Step philosophy offers some windows into spiritual development that you can use during your recovery from depression. Before discussing these ideas, read the Steps as written from a new perspective by Lewis Andrews, who has written a book on the application of the Twelve Steps to everyday living.

Step One: I have a problem that is causing me emotional distress.
Step Two: I know my Higher Power can take away my problem and restore my well-being.
Step Three: I give my problem to God.
Step Four: I look at my shortcomings as well as my good qualities as I try to cope with my problem.
Step Five: I confide these shortcomings and good qualities to another person.
Step Six: I ask myself if I am ready to have my shortcomings removed.
Step Seven: I humbly ask God to remove them.
Step Eight: As I try to cope with my problem, I acknowledge those I have harmed.

Step Nine: I am thinking of how I can change my actions and directly make up for harm I have caused others.

Step Ten: Every day I continue to look at how I am doing, and when I am wrong, I promptly admit it.

Step Eleven: I take a few moments every day to seek guidance from my Higher Power.

Step Twelve: I am grateful for what I have learned from this, and I use my new knowledge and insight to help someone else.

~

Here's one way to simplify and summarize these Steps: In Steps One, Two, and Three, you simply acknowledge both a need for help and a belief that help is possible. In Steps Four and Five, you look inward to see if anything is preventing you from growing. In Steps Six, Seven, and Eight, you build bridges with others to end your isolation. Steps Nine, Ten, and Eleven serve as reminders to "keep your house clean" so that problems will be less likely to develop. Step Twelve is a reminder to help others: most people find that reaching out to others helps them stay on solid ground.

Twelve Step philosophy contains important wisdom that can shed some light on recovery from depression. But keep in mind that working your Twelve Step program harder or better will probably not cure your depression any more than going to psychotherapy alone cures alcoholism. Here are some ways that using the Twelve Steps can help:

Step One

Think back to how you first understood your addiction in light of Step One. Before Step One, perhaps you believed you were in complete control of your alcohol or drug use, and that it didn't affect your life very much. In listening to others, and in thinking more about your own story, you learned how Step One applied to you.

Now think about your depression. Can you see ways that depression is beyond your control? Can you begin to accept that depression has a life of its own and that it has created unmanageability in your life?

Steps Two and Three

If you are depressed, it may feel as if the weight of the world is on your shoulders. You may feel alone and without support. Whom could you turn to for help? Whom could you trust, even if just a little? There are people who care and who can help. Are you willing to turn to them?

Steps Four and Five

In the depths of depression, people can become weighed down with guilt and despair as they attempt to do a Fourth Step inventory. When this happens, it's best to wait to postpone working on these Steps until you are in a better state of mind. That time will come.

However, you need not avoid these Steps altogether. If you are feeling ready, doing the Fourth and Fifth Steps with your depression in mind might help you begin to see the patterns of events that keep you stuck. Some people have important inner issues that need to be aired and left behind in Step Five. But take precautions. Choose to do "mini" Steps Four and Five, looking at just a few of your characteristics and leaving the rest for another time. Set time limits: don't spend more than a half hour a day on Step Four and plan to take your Fifth Step within a week or so at most. Finally, be sure to look at some of your positive characteristics and strengths. It's just as important to acknowledge them as it is to recognize the patterns that cause you pain. In summary, plan a brief, constructive visit through Steps Four and Five this time around. When your depression is past or reduced, you'll have time and strength to do these two Steps again. In general, many people find new ways of looking at the Twelve Steps and applying them to their lives at different points in time.

Steps Six and Seven

If you are depressed, you may believe that your shortcomings are unforgivable. You might think, *I'm not the person I could've been,* or, *It's no use; I've taken all the wrong turns in life.* But these Steps are a reminder to be human and let go of the past. It may be true that you have made grave mistakes, missed opportunities, or made choices that resulted in dead ends. You may be so mired in regrets that it is hard to have hope for the moment, much less the future. You can use Step Seven as a way to focus on the here and now and, "just for today," act as the person you want to be.

Steps Eight and Nine

These two Steps are an invitation to end the isolation of depression. Whom have you shut out? Have you blamed others for your depression? Again, don't use these Steps as an opportunity to beat yourself up. Try to keep recollections factual and simply acknowledge, "Yes, this is what has happened." Understand that depression, as a disorder, wreaks havoc on relationships with others; just when you need people the most, depression tells you (falsely) that connecting with others is not possible. Steps Eight and Nine can help you see, with clear eyes, the impact that depression may be having on your relationships. And these Steps give you a way to reclaim those relationships. (One of the most important relationships might be with yourself.)

Step Ten

In depression, you might be tempted to analyze your whole life and put a stamp of disapproval on it. But chances are good that, if looked at more closely, your life is a mixture of noble, loving moments as well as moments of blunders and missed opportunities. Depression somehow erases the good and puts the magnifying glass on the bad. Step Ten gives you a way to look at your day—and just this day—to see what's gone well and what has gone poorly. By doing so, you can give yourself credit where credit is due. And you can give yourself a framework for noticing things you are doing that help your recovery from depression, so the next day you may be able to do a little more in that same direction.

Step Eleven

When you are depressed, your mind may feel chaotic and confused. Negative thoughts may storm inside your head. When you try to direct your thoughts, you may feel that your mind seems to go blank. Step Eleven gives you the opportunity to still your mind. You can do this by sitting quietly in a special place and, just for twenty minutes, focusing on a candle, your own rhythm of breathing, or calming music. If thoughts intrude, you can quietly acknowledge them and gently tell them to go. There is no goal in this exercise, and you may not feel an immediate benefit. But over time, you may come to realize that you have made a space for stillness within you.

Step Twelve

As you work through your depression, you may find ways to be present for others who are struggling. While this *may* help the other person, it will *most certainly* help you. By reflecting, telling someone else how it was and how it is now, you are strengthening your own position beyond depression.

Depression and Twelve Step Programs

If you have been part of a Twelve Step group, continued involvement can be critical while you are depressed. In your group, you can still find a sense of community and support. Some days it may feel too hard to get yourself there. Or you might feel that you have very little to contribute. But it's still important to go! The very same things that support your recovery from addiction will also help you in your recovery from depression.

Some Alcoholics Anonymous or other Twelve Step groups are more comfortable with depression than others. (You also might consider checking out an Emotions Anonymous group.) If you find that members of your group are not as compassionate as you'd like, try not to take it personally. It reflects their understanding of depression more than it does your progress in overall recovery. You may need to be selective about which group members you talk to about your depression, or you may want to shop around for a group that feels more supportive. Either way, don't give up on yourself or the Twelve Steps.

The Twelve Steps that you've become familiar with in recovery from addiction can shed some light as you travel through depression. Try looking at the Steps in new ways, as Lewis Andrews has done in the earlier example (pages 239–240). Ask other people who are depressed and recovering from addiction what parts of the Twelve Step program have helped them. Again, don't fall into the trap of thinking that if you worked your program harder, you wouldn't be depressed! Be patient with yourself as you explore how you can find ways to grow in recovery from both addiction and depression.

What Does This Mean for Me?

Depression needs to be treated, often with a combination of psychotherapy and medication. At the same time, depression may bring some important messages. Sometimes people cannot understand the messages until they are safely out of the depths of despair. But at some point, it can be helpful to reflect back on what you have learned about yourself and how your life is richer for having traveled through depression.

Further Questions

If I need to see a therapist or get on medication for depression, does this mean that I've failed in my spiritual quest?

No, absolutely not. Depression is a disorder just as any other. If you developed heart disease, cancer, or a broken leg, you would probably not chastise yourself or believe that spiritual strength alone could prevent or correct these problems. Some people wait too long to get help with depression because they believe their spiritual work will sustain them or guide them through the depression. Spiritual beliefs and practices can certainly give you a guiding light, but treatment may also be necessary. Treatment for depression can actually help spiritual growth continue.

Who needs spirituality? If therapy and medication will take away my depression, why should I care about this spiritual stuff?

If treatment from depression can help spiritual growth continue, spiritual growth can also promote healing from depression. Most people who travel through depression have a profoundly changed view of themselves and their world. Finding ways to incorporate new knowledge into their lives can help people feel more solid within and more connected to their fellow human beings. In a simple way, this is spirituality.

What Can I Do to Help Myself?

Using some of the concepts of this chapter can help you see yourself and your depression in new ways. This in itself can produce movement and hope.

1. Imagine your depression as a bridge to new life and understanding. Sit with this image for a while. As you come back from your meditation, write or draw what you saw or felt. What was your bridge made of? Where did it take you? Were you alone or was someone you trusted with you? If you like, you can revisit this image anytime.

2. If you are coming out of your depression, you may be able to look back on wisdom you have gained from your experience. Take a piece of paper, and with full respect for yourself and your life, draw or write about some of the inner wisdom you have found.

3. In what ways have you been courageous in the face of depression? Maybe you resisted the idea of suicide. Maybe you found a way to reach out to someone else for help in spite of your fear and mistrust. Maybe you got up and out the door in the morning today even while feeling hopelessness and dread. These may be small or large victories that only you know about. But if you are surviving depression, you have been courageous.

For people in addiction recovery:

4. Which of the Twelve Steps were initially most helpful to you in your recovery from addiction? How can you apply them now to your depression?

5. Are you continuing to attend your regular Twelve Step meetings? If not, try to find ways to get yourself there. Could you call a friend and ask for a ride? Would it help to try a new meeting with new faces?

6. Is there anyone in your Twelve Step group whom you feel safe talking to about your depression? Have you talked to your sponsor about it? Do you feel it would be helpful if you did?

Appendix

A Brief Guide to Common Medications Used for Depression

If your doctor has prescribed a medication for your depression, you might have questions about it. This appendix gives you some basic information. Keep in mind, though, that it is only a general guide. You need to get specific, detailed information from your doctor or pharmacist, or from the written material that comes with your medication. The most important thing this section can do is to help you understand your own questions better and give you the courage to ask them.[1] Remember, there are no dumb questions about antidepressants.

Selective Serotonin Re-uptake Inhibitors (SSRIs) and Other Newer Antidepressants

Product name: Prozac
Chemical name: fluoxetine hydrochloride
How does Prozac work?

Current research indicates that depression is caused by a deficit of the neurotransmitter serotonin, one of the brain's natural mood-enhancing chemical messengers. Prozac works by blocking the re-uptake of serotonin, leaving more serotonin available.

What are the side effects?

Nausea, headache, insomnia, anxiety, nervousness, and drowsiness are the most common side effects of Prozac. Some people experience sexual difficulties, such as delayed orgasm or inability to have an orgasm; men may notice difficulty in maintaining erections.

What is the usual dose?

Typically, the initial dose is 20 mg/day, taken once in the morning. It takes six weeks to take full effect. The average effective dose is 20 to 30 mg/day; the highest recommended dose is 80 mg/day.

Product name: Zoloft
Chemical name: sertraline hydrochloride

How does Zoloft work?

Current research indicates that depression is caused by a deficit of the neurotransmitter serotonin, one of the brain's natural mood-enhancing chemical messengers. Zoloft works by blocking the re-uptake of serotonin, leaving more serotonin available.

What are the side effects?

The most common side effects of Zoloft are agitation, insomnia, ejaculatory delay, sleepiness, dizziness, headache, tremor, anorexia, diarrhea, nausea, and fatigue. Fifteen percent of depressed people given a prescription for Zoloft during studies discontinued its use due to adverse effects.

What is the usual dose?

Typically, the initial dose is 50 mg/day, once in the morning or evening. It takes several weeks to take full effect. The maximum dose is 200 mg/day.

Product name: Paxil
Chemical name: paroxetine

How does Paxil work?

Current research indicates that depression is caused by a deficit of the neurotransmitter serotonin, one of the brain's natural mood-enhancing chemical messengers. Paxil works by blocking the re-uptake of serotonin, leaving more serotonin available. Paxil is often prescribed to help decrease anxiety symptoms as well as depression.

What are the side effects?

The most common side effects of Paxil are weakness, sweating, nausea, constipation or diarrhea, sleepiness, dizziness, and insomnia; men may have problems with ejaculation. Most of these are dose-dependent; that is, the higher the dose, the more likely the side effect. Taking Paxil with food may reduce its gastrointestinal side effects. About 20 percent of people taking Paxil during its original studies discontinued use due to side effects.

What is the usual dose?

Typically, the initial dose is 20 mg/day, taken once in the morning. The maximum recommended dose is 50 mg/day. It takes two or more weeks to take full effect.

Unique Antidepressants

Product name: Desyrel, Trialodine, and Trazon
Chemical name: trazodone hydrochloride

How does trazodone work?

The mechanism of trazodone's antidepressant action in humans is not fully understood. It does appear to block the re-uptake of serotonin, thereby enhancing serotonin's effects. Trazodone decreases anxiety in people who are depressed and increases their sleep time. It is chemically unrelated to other antidepressants.

What are the side effects?

Drowsiness and fatigue are the major side effects of trazodone, occurring in 20 to 50 percent of patients, especially during the first few weeks. Dry mouth is also a common side effect. Some people experience changes in sexual function, for example, a decrease or increase in libido. For men, priapism (a persistent erection) can occur. Trazodone can cause orthostatic hypotension (decrease in blood pressure upon standing), and there have been case reports of cardiac arrhythmias in people with mitral valve prolapse and in people with and without family or personal history of heart disease.[2] Trazodone does not cause some of the side effects that are typical of tricyclics, for example, blurred vision, urinary retention, or constipation.

What is the usual dose?

Typically, the initial dose is 50 mg/day, taken three times a day. The maximum usual dose is 400 mg/day. It takes two or more weeks to take full effect. The dose is gradually tapered to the lowest dosage that is effective.

Product name: Effexor, Effexor XR
Chemical name: venlafaxine

How does Effexor work?

Effexor acts on both serotonin and norepinephrine, enhancing the action of both these neurotransmitters. It is prescribed for depression and related symptoms, such as anxiety.

What are the side effects?

The most common side effects of Effexor are short-term nausea, sleepiness, dry mouth, dizziness, constipation, nervousness, sweating, weakness, ejaculation or orgasm problems, and loss of appetite. Sustained levels of increased blood pressure and agitation can also occur.

What is the usual dose?

Typically, the initial dose is 75 to 375 mg/day. The average effective dose is usually between 125 and 150 mg/day. Some people divide it into two or three doses during the day and take it with food. It takes two or more weeks to take full effect.

What about use by pregnant women or nursing mothers?

Since Effexor is transmitted in breast milk, use during pregnancy and while nursing is not recommended.

Product name: Serzone
Chemical name: nefazodone

How does Serzone work?

Serzone appears to block the re-uptake of serotonin, thereby making the most of serotonin's effects. It was designed to be similar to trazodone, but without the effects of orthostatic hypotension and sedation.

What are the side effects?

Nausea, headache, and drowsiness were the most frequent side effects in clinical trials of Serzone. Feelings of weakness or dizziness also appeared in a significant portion of those taking the medication. It does not have the same level of side effects as the tricyclics, making it more favorable. Overall, about 16 percent of all those involved in premarketing trials of Serzone discontinued treatment due to side effects.

What is the usual dose?

Typically, the initial dose is 200 mg/day, taken in several doses during the day, and the usual effective dose is between 300 and 600 mg/day. It takes several weeks to take full effect. The dose is then gradually tapered to the lowest dosage that is effective.

Product name: Celexa
Chemical name: citalopram HBr

How does Celexa work?

Celexa selectively inhibits uptake of serotonin and is not related to any other SSRI or tricyclic.

What are the side effects?

Side effects include gastrointestinal problems, insomnia or sleepiness, dry mouth, tremor, and increased sweating. Men may experience ejaculation problems.

What is the usual dose?

Celaxa is taken once a day in the morning or evening, with or without food. The usual starting dose is 20 mg/day. It may be increased to 40 mg/day.

Product name: Remeron
Chemical name: mirtazapine

How does Remeron work?

Remeron is considered a tetracyclic compound that is not related to other classes of antidepressant drugs. The drug is prescribed for depression and associated symptoms, such as anxiety and difficulty in sleeping. Remeron has potent serotonergic and noradrenergic activity in the brain.

What are the side effects?

Drowsiness, increased appetite, weight gain, and dizziness. There are fewer sexual dysfunction side effects with this medication than with many other antidepressants.

What is the usual dose?

The effective dose range is 15 to 45 mg/day.

Tricyclic Antidepressants

Product name: Tofranil
Chemical name: imipramine

How does Tofranil work?

Tofranil blocks the re-uptake of several neurotransmitters. Tofranil is one of the tricyclic antidepressants, which are among the older antidepressant medications. People with a history of seizures, glaucoma, urinary retention, heart disease, or hyperthyroidism or people taking thyroid medicine should use the medication with extreme caution.

What are the side effects?

Side effects may include dry mouth and eyes, blurred vision, drowsiness, constipation, sensitivity to bright light, anxiety, night sweats, weight gain, and cardiovascular problems. Men may have trouble getting an erection or ejaculating.

What is the usual dose?

Typically, the initial dose is 50 to 75 mg/day, up to 150 to 200 mg/day. It can be taken all at once during the day or in up to four divided doses per day. It takes two or more weeks to take full effect. As soon as the depression abates, the dosage is tapered to the lowest dosage that is effective.

Product name: Elavil
Chemical name: amitriptyline hydrochloride

How does Elavil work?

Elavil, like other tricyclics, blocks the re-uptake of several neurotransmitters. It may help decrease anxiety in addition to reducing depression.

What are the side effects?

The side effects may include dry mouth and eyes, blurred vision, drowsiness, constipation, sensitivity to bright light, anxiety, night sweats, weight gain, and cardiovascular problems. Men may have trouble getting an erection or ejaculating.

What is the usual dose?

Typically, the initial dose is 50 to 200 mg/day, taken either once a day or in up to four divided doses daily. Some adults may be stabilized on 25 to 40 mg/day. It takes two or more weeks to take full effect. As soon as depression abates, the dosage is gradually tapered to the lowest dosage that is effective.

Product name: Aventyl and Pamelor
Chemical name: nortriptyline hydrochloride

How do Aventyl and Pamelor work?

They block the re-uptake of several neurotransmitters. They may help decrease anxiety.

What are the side effects?

The side effects of Aventyl and Pamelor may include dry mouth and eyes, blurred vision, drowsiness, constipation, sensitivity to bright light, anxiety, night sweats, weight gain, and cardiovascular problems. Men may have trouble getting an erection or ejaculating.

What is the usual dose?

Typically, the initial dose is 25 to 100 mg/day, taken either once a day or in up to four divided doses per day. It takes two or more weeks to take full effect. As soon as depression abates, the dosage is gradually tapered to the lowest dosage that is effective.

Product name: Norpramin
Chemical name: desipramine hydrochloride

How does Norpramin work?

Norpramin blocks the re-uptake of several neurotransmitters. It may help decrease anxiety in addition to reducing depression.

What are the side effects?

The side effects of Norpramin may include dry mouth and eyes, blurred vision, drowsiness, constipation, sensitivity to bright light, anxiety, night sweats, weight gain, and cardiovascular problems. Men may have trouble getting an erection or ejaculating.

What is the usual dose?

Typically, the initial dose is 50 to 300 mg/day, taken either once a day in the morning or at bedtime, or in up to three divided doses per day. It takes two or more weeks to take full effect. In some cases, the effect may be seen more rapidly, within two to five days. As soon as depression abates, the dosage is gradually tapered to the lowest dosage that is effective.

Product name: Sinequan
Chemical name: doxepin hydrochloride

How does Sinequan work?

Sinequan blocks the re-uptake of several neurotransmitters and has an anticholinergic effect. It may help decrease anxiety. It is also prescribed to help with anxiety that occurs with depression. In fact, a patient on Sinequan may feel a decrease in anxiety before experiencing a decrease in depression.

What are the side effects?

The side effects of Sinequan may include dry mouth and eyes, blurred vision, drowsiness, constipation, sensitivity to bright light, anxiety, night sweats, weight gain, cardiovascular problems. Men may have trouble getting an erection or ejaculating.

What is the usual dose?

Typically, the initial dose is 30 to 300 mg/day, taken either once a day in the morning or at bedtime, or in up to three divided doses per day. It takes two or more weeks to take full effect. As soon as depression abates, the dosage is gradually tapered to the lowest dosage that is effective.

Product name: Ludiomil
Chemical name: maprotiline hydrochloride

How does Ludiomil work?

Ludiomil appears to affect norepinephrine. It helps alleviate depression as well as anxiety. The *American Hospital Formulary* states that in studies done with Ludiomil and Elavil or Ludiomil and Tofranil, Ludiomil typically shows better results.[3]

What are the side effects?

The side effects of Ludiomil may include dry mouth, blurred vision, drowsiness, and constipation. Ludiomil may produce seizures more than other antidepressants.

What is the usual dose?

Typically, the initial dose is 75 to 150 mg/day, taken either once a day in the morning or at bedtime, or in up to three divided doses per day. It takes two or more weeks to take full effect. As soon as depression abates, the dosage is gradually tapered to the lowest dosage that is effective.

Product name: Asendin
Chemical name: amoxapine

How does Asendin work?

Asendin blocks the re-uptake of several neurotransmitters, particularly serotonin and norepinephrine. It may help decrease anxiety that accompanies depression.

What are the side effects?

The side effects of Asendin may include dry mouth and eyes, blurred vision, drowsiness, constipation, sensitivity to bright light, anxiety, night sweats, weight gain, and cardiovascular problems. Men may have trouble getting an erection or ejaculating. This medication, in rare cases, has been associated with tardive dyskinesia, a disorder of the nervous system that is caused by long-term use of a particular psychotropic medication.

What is the usual dose?

Typically, the initial dose is 100 to 300 mg/day, taken one to three times per day. (Single doses are usually taken at bedtime.) Usually it takes two or more weeks to take full effect, but for some people it works in as little as one week. As soon as depression abates, the dosage is gradually tapered to the lowest dosage that is effective.

Product name: Wellbutrin
Chemical name: bupropion hydrochloride

How does Wellbutrin work?

Wellbutrin is a weak blocker of serotonin and epinephrine, and (to some extent) dopamine.

What are the side effects?

Wellbutrin appears to produce seizures at a much higher rate—as much as four times higher—than other medications. Seizures are more likely in people who have anorexia or bulimia. It also produces more weight loss than other antidepressants. This medication produces less sexual dysfunction than some other antidepressants. Note that Wellbutrin contains the same ingredients as Zyban, a common prescription for quitting smoking. The two should never be taken together.

What is the usual dose?

Typically, the initial dose is 300 mg/day, taken three times a day: morning, noon, and night. It may take several weeks to take full effect.

What about use by alcoholics/addicts?

Wellbutrin "showed some increase in motor activity and agitation/excitement" and produced mild "amphetamine-like activity" among drug abusers in a research study.[4] The *Physician's Desk Reference* states that while research could not be done using higher doses (because of risk of seizures), "higher doses might be modestly attractive to those who abuse stimulant drugs." These cautions suggest that this antidepressant may not be advised for people who are recovering from addiction—or, if it is used, patient and doctor need to make sure that low doses are being used and any reinforcing effects are discussed.

Monoamine Oxidase Inhibitors (MAOIs)

Product name: Marplan
Chemical name: isocarboxazid

How does Marplan work?

Marplan inhibits the enzyme monoamine, which results in the increase of several amines, including serotonin, epinephrine, norepinephrine, and dopamine. It is used for people whose depression is not helped by other antidepressants.

What are the side effects?

The side effects of Marplan may include dizziness, weight gain, and drowsiness. The most serious problem is a possible hypertensive episode, a sudden increase in blood pressure that requires emergency treatment. A headache can be a warning sign. The episode can be precipitated by eating or drinking certain kinds of food or beverages, such as aged cheese, chocolate, alcohol, or caffeine, all of which contain a monoamine called tyramine. A patient must avoid a thorough list of foods, beverages, and medications.

What is the usual dose?

Typically, the initial dose is 10 to 30 mg/day, usually taken two times a day, morning and afternoon. Doses usually are not taken at bedtime, as some people experience insomnia. It usually takes three to four weeks to take full effect. Initially, a patient might be started on the highest dose (30 mg/day) and then backed down to a lower dose. Marplan accumulates in the body, so lower doses suffice to maintain positive effects.

What about use by alcoholics/addicts?

Because of this drug's low margin of safety, it is not considered safe for alcoholics.[5]

Product name: Nardil
Chemical name: phenelzine sulfate

How does Nardil work?

Nardil inhibits the enzyme monoamine, which results in the increase of several amines, including serotonin, epinephrine, norepinephrine, and dopamine. It is used for people whose depression is not helped by other antidepressants, particularly those who have depression with anxiety.

What are the side effects?

The side effects of Nardil may include dizziness, weight gain, and drowsiness. The most serious problem is a possible hypertensive episode, a sudden increase in blood pressure that requires emergency treatment. An episode can be precipitated by eating or drinking certain kinds of food or beverages, such as aged cheese, chocolate, alcohol, or caffeine. A patient should avoid a thorough list of foods, beverages, and medications.

What is the usual dose?

Typically, the initial dose is 15 to 90 mg/day, taken two or three times a day during the morning and afternoon. Doses usually are not taken at bedtime, as some people experience insomnia. It usually takes two to six weeks to take full effect. The medication is typically started at a medium dose (three doses of 15 mg), increased until maximum effect is achieved, and then slowly tapered to the lowest dosage that is effective.

What about use by alcoholics/addicts?

Because of this drug's low margin of safety, it is not considered safe for alcoholics.[6]

Product name: Parnate
Chemical name: tranylcypromine sulfate

How does Parnate work?

Parnate inhibits an enzyme called monoamine, which results in the increase of several amines, including serotonin, epinephrine, norepinephrine, and dopamine. This MAOI produces greater stimulation than other MAOIs and takes effect more quickly.

What are the side effects?

The side effects of Parnate may include agitation, dizziness, weight gain, and drowsiness. The most serious problem is a possible hypertensive episode, a sudden increase in blood pressure that requires emergency treatment. An episode can be precipitated by eating or drinking certain kinds of food or beverages, such as aged cheese, chocolate, alcohol, or caffeine. A patient should avoid a thorough list of foods, beverages, and medications. Withdrawal symptoms, such as weakness, diarrhea, anxiety, and confusion, can also occur when it is discontinued.

What is the usual dose?

Typically, the initial dose is 30 to 60 mg/day, taken two times a day, in the morning and afternoon. Doses usually are not taken at bedtime, as some people experience insomnia. It usually takes two to three weeks to take full effect. Parnate has a more complex pharmacological action than other MAOIs, and patients taking it may need to work closely with their physicians, especially at the beginning, to determine appropriate doses.

What about use by alcoholics/addicts?

Because of its special characteristics (fast-acting, stimulant effects and withdrawal symptoms), Parnate is not recommended for alcoholics or addicts. The *Physician's Desk Reference* states: "There have been reports of drug dependency in patients using doses of tranylcypromine (Parnate) significantly in excess of the therapeutic range. Some of these patients had a history of previous substance abuse."[7] Because of this drug's low margin of safety, it is not considered safe for alcoholics.[8]

Mood Stabilizers

Product name: lithium
Chemical name: lithium salts

Lithium is one of the first drugs used for treating manic episodes. Its usefulness in treating manic episodes was discovered serendipitously by an Australian psychiatrist named John Cade in 1948.

How does lithium work?

Lithium is in a special category of its own and is used in treating and preventing episodes of depression and mania in people with bipolar disorder. It has the effect of reducing the wide fluctuations of mood in bipolar disorder. It can also be used to treat recurrent depression without mania. Since lithium has many complex chemical effects, how it works is not well understood. It does appear to affect neurotransmitters that are involved in depression and mania.

What are the side effects?

Lethargy, muscle weakness, fatigue, and hand tremors are the most frequent side effects of lithium. Nausea and diarrhea may also occur.

What is the usual dose?

Lithium comes in several forms (regular pills, extended release tablets [such as Lithobid], or liquid), and the dose depends on the form. Blood levels are taken when a person first begins lithium, when any changes are made, and periodically over time in order to determine whether lithium is at a therapeutic level.

What about use by alcoholics/addicts?

In the 1970s and 1980s, there was hope that lithium could be used to help alcoholics stop drinking. More rigorous research in the 1980s showed this not to be true. In most studies, use of lithium among depressed alcoholics did not decrease alcohol intake. Surprisingly, the same research showed that lithium did not improve depression among alcoholics. (However, these alcoholics were in early recovery.) Research has not been done on the effects of lithium specifically on manic-depressive symptoms of alcoholics or addicts, but it is assumed to be as effective as it is with people who are not drug dependent.

Lithium is often used in combination with other drugs; in general, mixtures of lithium and Depakote (valproate) are most common.

The combination of lithium and Depakote is often used in bipolar illness and may be especially helpful for those who have rapid cycles (more than four per year). Some impressive research results have demonstrated this combination's efficacy. For example, in one study, patients receiving lithium and Depakote were less likely to have a relapse during the year of follow-up than patients taking a combination of Depakote and a placebo.[9]

Lithium and carbamazepine is another common combination for treating bipolar illness, though the use of Depakote rather than carbamazepine is increasing. Carbamazepine may have more side effects in some patients, and it may be harder to regulate in its interactions with other drugs. However, many studies have shown good results in resolving manic episodes and in preventing future episodes.[10]

Combinations of lithium and calcium channel blockers (such as verapamil, diltiazem, nifedipine), while appearing promising in earlier research, are not considered to be safe.[11]

Product name: Depakote
Chemical name: valproate

How does Depakote work?

Depakote is often used in combination with lithium as a treatment for manic episodes. It may be most helpful for patients with rapid cycles.

The combination of Depakote and carbamazepine is generally not recommended; though often found to be effective, there are important safety considerations. Blood monitoring is essential during use of this combination, as there are synergistic effects between the two drugs.[12]

What are the side effects?

Nausea, sleepiness, and dizziness. Safety considerations include problems in liver functioning.

What is the usual dose?

Initially, 750 mg/day in divided doses, reduced every two to three days to the lowest effective level and desired plasma level. The maximum recommended dosage is 60 milligrams per kilogram (of body weight) per day.

What about use by pregnant women or nursing mothers?

Use during pregnancy and nursing is not recommended, as Depakote may produce birth defects such as spina bifida.

Product name: Tegretol
Chemical name: carbamazepine

How does Tegretol work?

Tegretol is useful as an anticonvulsant and analgesic, but it is also effective for some people in controlling manic episodes and bipolar disorder. It may be used alone or in combination with lithium. Tegretol's most important action is to reduce some nerve cell activity in the brain ("postsynaptic")—thereby reducing seizures. But it is not known how this action produces mood stabilization.

What are the side effects?

The most serious side effects of Tegretol may include changes in the circulatory system, heart, kidneys, and liver. Although effects on these systems are not common, they can be dangerous. Because of this, it is especially important to work with a physician familiar with Tegretol and its use.

What is the usual dose?

Patients are started at a low dose and the dose is slowly increased to the most therapeutic levels. The dosage depends on the form of the drug (pills or liquid) and the nature of a patient's problems.

The Twelve Steps of Alcoholics Anonymous*

1. We admitted we were powerless over alcohol—that our lives had become unmanageable.
2. Came to believe that a Power greater than ourselves could restore us to sanity.
3. Made a decision to turn our will and our lives over to the care of God *as we understood Him.*
4. Made a searching and fearless moral inventory of ourselves.
5. Admitted to God, to ourselves, and to another human being the exact nature of our wrongs.
6. Were entirely ready to have God remove all these defects of character.
7. Humbly asked Him to remove our shortcomings.
8. Made a list of all persons we had harmed, and became willing to make amends to them all.
9. Made direct amends to such people wherever possible, except when to do so would injure them or others.
10. Continued to take personal inventory and when we were wrong promptly admitted it.
11. Sought through prayer and meditation to improve our conscious contact with God *as we understood Him,* praying only for knowledge of His will for us and the power to carry that out.
12. Having had a spiritual awakening as the result of these steps, we tried to carry this message to alcoholics, and to practice these principles in all our affairs.

---

*The Twelve Steps of Alcoholics Anonymous are taken from *Alcoholics Anonymous,* 3d ed., published by AA World Services, Inc., New York, N.Y., 59–60. Reprinted with permission of AA World Services, Inc. (See editor's note on copyright page.)

Resources

National Institute of Mental Health
6001 Executive Blvd., Rm. 8184, MSC 9663
Bethesda, MD 20892-9663
Phone: 301-443-4513
www.nimh.nih.gov/publicat/depressionmenu.cfm

SA\VE (Suicide Awareness\Voices of Education)
P.O. Box 24507
Minneapolis, MN 55424-0507
Phone: 612-946-7998
Emergency phone: 1-800-SUICIDE
www.save.org

National Depressive and Manic-Depressive Association
730 N. Franklin Street, Suite 501
Chicago, IL 60610-3526
Phone: 1-800-826-3632
www.ndmda.org

American Association for Retired People (AARP)
601 E Street NW
Washington, DC 20049
Phone: 1-800-424-3410
www.aarp.org/griefandloss

National Alliance for the Mentally Ill
Colonial Place Three
2107 Wilson Blvd., Suite 300
Arlington, VA 22201-3042
Phone: 1-800-950-6264
www.nami.org

National Foundation for Depressive Illness, Inc.
P.O. Box 2257
New York, NY 10116
Phone: 1-800-239-1265
www.depression.org

Notes

Chapter 1: What Is Depression?

1. American Psychiatric Association, *Diagnostic and Statistical Manual of Mental Disorders*, 4th ed. (Washington, D.C.: American Psychiatric Association, 1994), 317–93. See also *Supplement to American Journal of Psychiatry* 150, no. 4 (1993).

2. P. F. Sullivan, R. C. Kessler, and K. S. Kendler, "Latent Class Analysis of Lifetime Depressive Symptoms in the National Comorbidity Survey," *American Journal of Psychiatry* 155 (1998): 1398–1406.

3. J. C. Markowitz, "Psychotherapy of Dysthymia," *American Journal of Psychiatry* 151, no. 8 (1994): 114–21.

4. J. A. Flint and S. L. Rifat, "Two-Year Outcome of Psychotic Depression in Late Life," *American Journal of Psychiatry* 155 (1998): 178–83.

5. L. Tondo and R. J. Baldessarini, "Rapid Cycling in Women and Men with Bipolar Manic-Depressive Disorders," *American Journal of Psychiatry* 155 (1998): 1434–36.

6. C. Salzman, "Integrating Pharmacotherapy and Psychotherapy in the Treatment of a Bipolar Patient," *American Journal of Psychiatry* 155 (1998): 686–88.

7. N. E. Rosenthal, *Winter Blues* (New York: Guilford Press, 1993), 29–39.

8. A. T. F. Beekman, E. deBeurs, A. J. van Balkom, D. J.

Deeg, R. van Dyck, and W. van Tilburg, "Anxiety and Depression in Later Life: Co-occurrence and Communality of Risk Factors," *American Journal of Psychiatry* 157 (2000): 89–95.

9. S. A. Brown, R. K. Inaba, J. C. Gillin, M. A. Schuckit, M. A. Stewart, and M. R. Irwin, "Alcoholism and Affective Disorder: Clinical Course of Depressive Symptoms," *American Journal of Psychiatry* 152, no. 1 (1995): 45–52.

10. M. A. Schuckit, "Alcohol, Anxiety and Depressive Disorders," *Alcohol Health and Research World* 20, no. 2 (1996): 81–85.

11. J. E. Helzer and T. R. Pryzbeck, "The Co-occurrence of Alcoholism with Other Psychiatric Disorders in the General Population and Its Impact on Treatment," *Journal of Studies on Alcohol* 49, no. 3 (1998): 219–24.

12. Centers for Disease Control. Available at www.cdc.gov/nchs/fastats/suicide.htm

13. K. S. Kendler and C. O. Gardner, "Boundaries of Major Depression: An Evaluation of DSMIV Criteria," *American Journal of Psychiatry* 155 (1998): 172–77.

Chapter 2: Who Has Depression?

1. K. Cronkite, *On the Edge of Darkness: Conversations about Conquering Depression* (New York: Delta, 1995).

2. W. Styron, *Darkness Visible: A Memoir of Madness* (New York: Vintage Books, 1992).

3. "A Patient's Perspective—Dick Cavett," *Smooth Sailing* (Spring 1992). Available on-line at www.ww2.med.jhu.edu/drada/cavett.html (accessed June 26, 2000).

4. J. Collins, *Singing Lessons: A Memoir of Love, Loss, Hope and Healing* (New York: Pocket Books, 1998).

5. R. C. Kessler, K. A. McGonagle, and Z. Shanyang, "Lifetime and 12-Month Prevalence of DSMIII-R Psychiatric Disorders in the United States," *Archives of General Psychiatry*, 51 (1994): 8–19.

6. Ibid.

7. D. G. Blazer, R. C. Kessler, K. A. McGonagle, and M. S. Schwartz, "The Prevalence and Distribution of Major Depression in a National Community Sample: The National Comorbidity Study," *American Journal of Psychiatry* 151, no. 7 (1994): 979–86.

8. E. L. Bassuk, J. C. Buckner, J. N. Perloff, and S. S. Bassuk, "Prevalence of Mental Health and Substance Use Disorders among Homeless and Low-Income Housed Mothers," *American Journal of Psychiatry* 155 (1998): 1561–64.

9. Kessler, McGonagle, and Shanyang, "Lifetime and 12-Month Prevalence of DSMIII-R Psychiatric Disorders in the United States." (See note 5, page 274.)

10. Ibid.

11. D. T. Takeuchi, R. C. Chung, K. Lin, H. Shen, K. Kurasaki, C. Chun, and S. Sue, "Lifetime and Twelve-Month Prevalence Rates of Major Depressive Episodes and Dysthymia among Chinese Americans in Los Angeles," *American Journal of Psychiatry* 155 (1998): 1407–14.

12. Kessler, McGonagle, and Shanyang, "Lifetime and 12-Month Prevalence of DSMIII-R Psychiatric Disorders in the United States." (See note 5, page 274.)

13. Ibid.

14. B. G. Druss, R. M. Rohrbaugh, and R. A. Rosenheck, "Depressive Symptoms and Health Costs in Older Medical Patients," *American Journal of Psychiatry* 156 (1999): 477–79.

15. Blazer et al., "The Prevalence and Distribution of Major Depression in a National Community Sample." (See note 7.)

16. "Depression and Healthcare: The High Cost of Saving," *Mind Body Health Newsletter* 5, no. 2 (1996): 7.

17. J. Unutzer, D. L. Patrick, G. Simon, D. Grembowski, E. Walker, C. Rutter, and W. Katon, "Depressive Symptoms and the Cost of Health Services in HMO Patients Aged 65 Years and Older," *Journal of the American Medical Association* 277 (1997):

1618–23; M. S. Pallak, N. A. Cummings, H. Dorken, and C. J. Henken, "Effects of Mental Health Treatment on Medical Costs," *Mind/Body Medicine* 1, no. 1 (1995): 7–12.

18. H. E. Ross, F. B. Glaser, and T. Germanson, "The Prevalence of Mental Disorders in Patients with Alcohol and Other Drug Problems," *Archives of General Psychiatry* 45 (1998): 977–85.

Chapter 3: What Causes Depression?

1. American Psychiatric Association, *Diagnostic and Statistical Manual of Mental Disorders*, 4th ed. (Washington, D.C.: American Psychiatric Association, 1994), 342, 348, 354, 361.

2. L. Grinspoon and J. B. Bakalar, "Depression and Other Mood Disorders," *The Harvard Medical School Mental Health Review* (1990).

3. L. J. Bierut, A. C. Heath, K. K. Bucholz, S. H. Dinwiddlie, P. A. F. Madden, D. J. Statham, M. P. Dunne, and N. G. Martin, "Major Depressive Disorder in a Community-Based Twin Sample," *Archives of General Psychiatry* 56 (1999): 557–63.

4. Ibid.

5. J. W. Wetzel, *Clinical Handbook of Depression* (New York: Gardner Press, 1984).

6. "Mental Health: A Report of the Surgeon General," Department of Health and Human Services (1999). Available at www.surgeongeneral.gov/library/mentalhealth.

7. C. B. Nemeroff, "The Neurobiology of Depression," *Scientific American* (June 1998): 142–49.

8. Ibid.

9. Ibid.

10. D. Liu, J. Dorio, B. Tannenbaum, C. Caldju, D. Francis, A. Freedman, S. Sharma, D. Pearson, P. M. Plotsky, and M. J. Meaney, "Maternal Care, Hippocampal Glucocorotid Receptors, and Hypothalmic–Pituitary–Adrenal Responses to Stress, " *Science* 277 (1997): 1659–62.

11. Nemeroff, "The Neurobiology of Depression." (See note 7, page 276.)

12. Grinspoon and Bakalar, "Depression and Other Mood Disorders." (See note 2, page 276.)

13. Wetzel, *Clinical Handbook of Depression*. (See note 5, page 276).

14. R. D. Levitan, S. V. Parikh, A. D. Lesage, K. M. Hegadoren, M. Adams, S. H. Kennedy, and P. N. Goering, "Major Depression in Individuals with a History of Childhood Physical or Sexual Abuse: Relationship to Neurovegetative Features, Mania, and Gender," *American Journal of Psychiatry* 155 (1998): 1746–52.

15. C. Swett and M. Halpert, "High Rates of Alcohol Problems and History of Physical and Sexual Abuse among Women Inpatients," *American Journal of Drug and Alcohol Abuse* 20 (1994): 263–72.

16. A. Y. Shalev, S. Freedman, T. Peri, D. Brandes, T. Sahar, S. P. Orr, and R. K. Pitman, "Prospective Study of Posttraumatic Stress Disorder and Depression Following Trauma," *American Journal of Psychiatry* 155 (1998): 630–37.

17. M. E. P. Seligman, *Learned Optimism* (New York: Pocket Books, 1999).

18. American Association of Hospital Pharmacists, *American Hospital Formulary Service Drug Information* (Bethesda, Md.: American Association of Hospital Pharmacists, 1993), 1927.

19. American Psychiatric Association, *Practice Guideline for Major Depressive Disorder in Adults* (Washington, D.C.: American Psychiatric Press, 1993).

20. K. Deater-Deckard, K. Pickering, J. F. Dunn, J. Golding, and the Avon Longitudinal Study of Childhood and Pregnancy Study Team, "Family Structure and Depressive Symptoms in Men Preceding and Following the Birth of a Child," *American Journal of Psychiatry* 155 (1998): 818–23.

21. Ibid.

22. American Psychiatric Association, *Diagnostic and Statistical Manual*, 717. (See note 1, page 276.)

23. R. F. Anda, D. F. Williamson, L. G. Escobedo, E. E. Mast, G. A. Giovino, and P. L. Remington, "Depression and the Dynamics of Smoking," *Journal of American Medical Association* 264, no. 12 (1999): 1541–45.

24. S. M. Hall, R. F. Munoz, V. I. Reus, and K. L. Sees, "Nicotine, Negative Affect and Depression," *Journal of Consulting and Clinical Psychology* 61, no. 5 (1993): 761–67.

25. M. L. Parchman, "Recognition of Depression in Patients Who Smoke," *Journal of Family Practice* 33 (1991): 255–58.

26. D. M. Wright and P. P. Heppner, "Coping among Nonclinical College-Age Children of Alcoholics," *Journal of Counseling Psychology* 38, no. 4 (1991): 465–72; National Institute on Alcohol Abuse and Alcoholism, "Children of Alcoholics: Are They Different?" *Alcohol Alert* (Rockville, Md.: National Institute on Alcohol Abuse and Alcoholism, 1990); M. O. West and R. J. Prinz, "Parental Alcoholism and Childhood Psychopathology," *Psychological Bulletin* 102, no. 2 (1987): 204–18.

27. W. Coryell, G. Winokur, M. Keller, W. Scheftner, and J. Endicott, "Alcoholism and Primary Major Depression: A Family Study Approach to Co-existing Disorders," *Journal of Affective Disorders* 24 (1992): 93–99; G. Winokur, R. Cadoret, J. Dorzel, and M. Baker, "Depressive Disease: A Genetic Study," *Archives of General Psychiatry* 24 (1971): 135–44.

28. J. B. Gross, "Clinician's Guide to Hepatitis C," *Mayo Clinic Proceedings* 78 (1998): 355–61.

29. S. Deb, I. Lyons, C. Koutzoukis, I. Ali, and G. McCarthy, "Rate of Psychiatric Illness One Year after Traumatic Brain Injury," *American Journal of Psychiatry* 156 (1999): 374–78.

30. N. E. Rosenthal, *Winter Blues* (New York: Guilford Press, 1993), 29–39; D. A. Oren, D. E. Moul, P. J. Schwartz, C. Brown,

E. M. Yamada, and N. E. Rosenthal, "Exposure to Ambient Light in Patients with Winter Seasonal Affective Disorder," *American Journal of Psychiatry* 151, no. 4 (1994): 591–93.

31. American Psychiatric Association, *Diagnostic and Statistical Manual*, 370–75. (See note 1, page 276.)

32. B. F. Grant and D. A. Dawson, "Alcohol and Drug Use, Abuse, and Dependence: Classification, Prevalence, and Co-morbidity," in *Addiction: A Comprehensive Guidebook*, ed. B. S. McCrady and E. E. Epstein (New York: Oxford University Press, 1999), 9–29; R. S. Stephens, "Cannabis and Hallucinogens," in *Addiction: A Comprehensive Guidebook*, 121–40.

33. R. A. Brown, P. M. Monti, M. G. Myers, R. A. Martin, T. Rivinus, M. E. Dubreuil, and D. J. Rohsenow, "Depression among Cocaine Abusers in Treatment: Relation to Cocaine and Alcohol Use and Treatment Outcome," *American Journal of Psychiatry* 155 (1998): 220–25.

34. D. G. Blazer, R. C. Kessler, K. A. McGonagle, and M. S. Schwartz, "The Prevalence and Distribution of Major Depression in a National Community Sample: The National Comorbidity Study," *American Journal of Psychiatry* 151, no. 7 (1994): 979–86; R. C. Kessler, K. A. McGonagle, and Z. Shanyang, "Lifetime and 12-Month Prevalence of DSMIII-R Psychiatric Disorders in the United States," *Archives of General Psychiatry* 51 (1994): 8–19.

35. S. S. Covington and J. L. Surrey, "The Relational Model of Women's Psychological Development: Implications for Substance Abuse," in *Gender and Alcohol*, ed. J. Wilsnack and R. Wilsnack (Piscataway, N.J.: Rutgers University, 1994).

36. L. S. Covey, A. H. Glassman, F. Stetner, and J. Becker, "Effect of History of Alcoholism or Major Depression on Smoking Cessation," *American Journal of Psychiatry* 150, no. 10 (1997): 1546–47.

37. Wright and Heppner, "Coping among Nonclinical College-Age Children of Alcoholics." (See note 26, page 278.)

Chapter 4: Depression and Death

1. "Suicide in the United States," Centers for Disease Control. Available at www.cdc.gov/ncipc/factsheets/suifacts.htm

2. "Suicide among Black Youths," Centers for Disease Control. Available at www.cdc.gov/od/oc/media/fact/suicidby.htm

3. B. Bongar, *The Suicidal Patient: Clinical and Legal Standards of Care* (Washington, D.C.: American Psychological Association, 1991).

4. W. Styron, *Darkness Visible: A Memoir of Madness* (New York: Vintage Books, 1990).

5. G. E. Valliant, "Natural History of Male Psychological Health, XIV: Relationship of Mood Disorder Vulnerability to Physical Health," *American Journal of Psychiatry* 155 (1998): 184–91.

6. B. W. Pennix, S. W. Geerlings, D. J. Deeg, J. T. van Eijk, W. van Tilburg, "Minor and Major Depression and the Risk of Death in Older Persons," *Archives of General Psychiatry* 56 (1999): 864–74.

7. A. H. Glassman, J. E. Helzer, L. S. Covey, L. B. Cottler, F. Stetner, J. E. Tipp, and J. Johnson, "Smoking, Smoking Cessation, and Major Depression," *Journal of the American Medical Association* 264 (1990): 1546–49.

8. A. H. Glassman and P. A. Shapiro, "Depression and the Course of Coronary Artery Disease," *American Journal of Psychiatry* 155, no.1 (1998): 4–11.

9. T. Maruta, R. C. Colligan, M. Malinchoc, and K. P. Offord, "Optimists vs. Pessimists: Survival Rate among Medical Patients over a 30-Year Period," *Mayo Clinic Proceedings* 75, no. 2 (February 2000).

10. C. B. Barrick, "Sad, Glad, or Mad Hearts? Epidemiological Evidence from a Causal Relationship between Mood Disorders and Coronary Artery Disease," *Journal of Affective Disorders* 53 (1999): 193–201.

11. Ibid.

12. Glassman and Shapiro, "Depression and the Course of Coronary Artery Disease." (See note 8, page 280.)

Chapter 5: What Can I Do about My Depression? Psychotherapy

1. A. T. Beck, A. J. Rush, B. F. Shaw, and G. Emery, *Cognitive Therapy for Depression* (New York: Guilford Press, 1979), 386–96; G. A. Fava, S. Grandi, M. Zielezny, R. Canestrari, and M. A. Morphy, "Cognitive Behavioral Treatment of Residual Symptoms in Primary Major Depressive Disorder," *American Journal of Psychiatry* 151, no. 9 (1994): 1295–329.

2. D. D. Burns, *Feeling Good: The New Mood Therapy* (New York: Signet Books, 1980).

3. R. J. DeRubeis, L. A. Gelfand, T. Z. Tang, and A. Simon, "Medications versus Cognitive Behavioral Therapy for Severely Depressed Outpatients," *American Journal of Psychiatry* 156 (1999): 1007–13.

4. W. Glasser, *Reality Therapy* (New York: Harper and Row, 1965).

5. J. O. Prochaska, C. C. DiClimente, and J. C. Norcross, "In Search of How People Change: Applications to Addictive Behaviors," *American Journal of Psychology* 47, no. 9 (1992): 1102–14; J. O. Prochaska, J. S. Rossi, and N. S. Wilcox, "Change Processes and Psychotherapy Outcome in Integrative Case Research," *Journal of Psychotherapy Integration* 1, no. 2 (1991): 103–20.

6. Prochaska, DiClemente, and Norcross, "In Search of How People Change." (See note 5.)

7. Ibid.

Chapter 6: What Can I Do about My Depression? Lifestyle

1. G. Parker, S. Itadzi, and D. Pavlovic, "Modification of Levels of Depression in Mother-Bereaved Women by Parental

and Marital Relationships," *Psychological Medicine* 14 (1984): 125–35.

2. J. M. Lewis, "For Better or Worse: Interpersonal Relationships and Individual Outcome," *American Journal of Psychiatry* 155 (1998): 582–89.

3. M. Seligman, "Positive Psychology: An Introduction," *American Psychologist* 55 (2000): 5–14.

4. M. Seligman, *Learned Optimism: How to Change Your Mind and Your Life* (New York: Pocket Books, 1998).

5. A. D. Kogan and P. M. Guilford, "Side Effects of Short Term 10,000 Lux Light Therapy," *American Journal of Psychiatry* 155 (1998): 293–94; R. D. Levitan, N. A. Rector, and M. Bagby, "Negative Attributional Style in Seasonal and Nonseasonal Depression," *American Journal of Psychiatry* 155 (1998): 428–30.

6. T. Postolache, T. A. Hardin, F. S. Myers, E. H. Turner, L. Y. Yo, R. L. Barnett, F. R. Matthers, and N. E. Rosenthal, "Greater Improvement in Summer than with Light Treatment in Winter in Patients with Seasonal Affective Disorder," *American Journal of Psychiatry* 155 (1998): 1614–16.

7. Kogan and Guilford, "Side Effects of Short Term 10,000 Lux Light Therapy." (See note 5.)

8. L. Lamberg, "Dawn's Early Light to Twilight's Last Gleaming," *Journal of American Medical Association* 11 (1988): 1556–58.

9. Ibid.

10. Ibid.

11. T. G. Plante, "Aerobic Exercise in the Prevention and Treatment of Psychopathology," in *Exercise Psychology: The Influence of Physical Exercise on Psychological Processes,* ed. P. Seraganian (New York: John Wiley & Sons, 1993), 358–79; T. G. Plante and J. Rodin, "Physical Fitness and Enhanced Psychological Health," *Current Psychology: Research & Reviews* 9, no. 1 (1990): 3–24.

12. M. Kavussanu and E. McAuley, "Exercise and Optimism: Are Highly Active Individuals More Optimistic?" *Journal of Sport & Exercise Psychology* 17 (1995): 246–58.

13. D. Greenberg and C. Oglesby, "President's Council on Physical Fitness and Sports Report: Mental Health Dimensions" (1997). Available at www.kls.coled.umn.edu/crgws/pcpfs/sxn4.html

14. Ibid.

15. Press release, "Duke Study: Exercise May Be Just as Effective as Medication for Treating Major Depression," Duke University, 24 October 1999. Available at www.dukenews.duke.edu/Med/nopills.htm; J. A. Blumenthal, M. A. Babyak, K. A. Moore, W. E. Craighead, S. Herman, P. Khatri, R. Waugh, M. A. Napolitano, L. M. Forman, M. Applebaum, P. M. Doraiswamy, and K. R. Krishnan, "Effects of Exercise Training on Older Patients with Major Depression," *Archives of Internal Medicine* 159 (1999): 2349–56.

16. M. Artal and C. A. Sherman, "Exercise Against Depression," *The Physician and Sportsmedicine* 26, no. 10 (October 1998). Available at www.physsportsmed.com/issues/1998/10Oct/artal/htm

17. S. N. Young, "The Use of Diet and Dietary Components in the Study of Factors Controlling Affect in Humans: A Review," *Journal of Psychiatry and Neuroscience* 18 (1993): 235–44.

18. J. Brody, *Good Food Book* (New York: Bantam Books, 1985).

19. Young, "The Use of Diet and Dietary Components," 235–44. (See note 17.)

20. Brody, *Good Food Book*. (See note 18.)

21. M. Peet, B. Murphy, J. Shay, and D. Horrotin, "Depletion of Omega 3 Fatty Acids in Red Blood Cell Membranes of Depressive Patients," *Biological Psychiatry* 43 (1998): 315–19.

22. A. L. Stoll, E. Steverus, M. P. Freeman, S. Reuter, H. A. Zboyan, E. Diamond, K. K. Dress, and L. B. Mangaell, "Omega 3

Fatty Acids in Bipolar Disorder," *Archives of General Psychiatry* 56 (1999): 407–12; J. R. Calabrese, D. J. Rapport, and M. D. Shelton, "Fish Oils and Bipolar Disorder," *Archives of General Psychiatry* 56 (1999): 413–14.

Chapter 7: What Can I Do about My Depression? Antidepressant Medication

1. Sambunaris, J. K. Hesselink, R. Pinder, J. Pangides, and S. M. Stahl, "Development of New Antidepressants," *Journal of Clinical Psychiatry* 5, no. 6 (1997): 40–52.

2. Ibid.

3. R. C. Rosen, R. M. Lane, and M. Menza, "Effects of SSRIs on Sexual Function: A Critical Review," *Journal of Clinical Psychopharmacology* 19, no. 1 (February 1999): 67–85.

4. M. E. Thase and D. J. Kupfer, "Recent Developments in the Pharmacotherapy of Mood Disorders," *Journal of Consulting and Clinical Psychology* 64 (1999): 646–59.

5. M. Konner, "Out of the Darkness," *The New York Times Magazine* (October 1994): 71–73.

6. B. Pepper, personal communication (December 1994).

7. J. F. Greden, "Understanding and Treating Major Depressive Illness," *Advances in Psychiatric Medicine,* supplement to the *Psychiatric Times,* ed. R. W. Pies (September 1994)

8. F. Therrien and J. S. Markowitz, "Selective Serotonin Re-uptake Inhibitors and Withdrawal Symptoms: A Review of the Literature," *Human Psychopharmacology* 12 (1997): 309–23.

9. Ibid.

10. J. Forman, "St. John's Wort, Antidepressants Don't Mix," *Boston Globe,* reprinted in *Minneapolis Star Tribune,* Sunday, 23 January 2000.

11. Ibid.

12. R. Fukushima, "Can SAM-e Beat the Blues?" *Saint Paul Pioneer Press,* 16 August 1999.

13. W. S. Appleton, *Prozac and the New Antidepressants* (New York: Penguin, 2000).

14. Sambunaris, Hesselink, Pinder, Pangides, and Stahl, "Development of New Antidepressants." (See note 1, page 284.)

15. Ibid.

16. Alcoholics Anonymous, *The A.A. Member: Medications and Other Drugs*, rev. ed. (New York: Alcoholics Anonymous World Services, 1994).

17. Alcoholics Anonymous, *'Pass It On,' The Story of Bill Wilson and How the A.A. Message Reached the World* (New York: Alcoholics Anonymous World Services, 1984), 292–303.

18. Ibid.

19. N. Wing, *Grateful to Have Been There* (Park Ridge, Ill.: Parkside Publishing Company, 1992), 53–55; Alcoholics Anonymous, *As Bill Sees It: Selected Writings of AA's Co-founder* (New York: Alcoholics Anonymous World Services, 1967), 30.

20. Ibid.

21. R. Z. Litten and J. P. Allen, "Pharmacotherapy for Alcoholics with Collateral Depression or Anxiety: An Update of Research Findings," *Experimental and Clinical Pharmacology* 3, no. 1 (1995): 87–93.

22. U.S. Department of Health and Human Services, Public Health Service, *Depression Is a Treatable Illness: A Patient's Guide* (April 1993).

23. Ibid.

24. C. Holden, "Depression: The News Isn't Depressing," *Science* 254 (1991): 1450–52.

25. B. Pepper, personal communication (December 1994).

26. A. A. Nierenberg, L. A. Adler, E. Peselow, G. Zornberg, and M. Rosenthal, "Trazodone for Antidepressant-Associated Insomnia," *Archives of General Psychiatry* 151 (7): 1069–72.

27. L. McGinley, "Lilly's Prozac Is Cleared by FDA to Treat Bulimia," *Wall Street Journal*, 27 April 1994.

Chapter 8: Depression and the Family

1. P. D. Kramer, *Listening to Prozac* (New York: Penguin Group, 1993).

2. W. Styron, *Darkness Visible: A Memoir of Madness* (New York: Random House, 1990), 77.

Chapter 9: Depression as a Spiritual Phenomenon

1. E. A. Peers, *Dark Night of the Soul by St. John of the Cross* (New York: Image Books, 1990).

2. R. S. Anderson and P. Hopkins, *The Feminine Face of God* (New York: Bantam Books, 1991).

3. W. Styron, *Darkness Visible: A Memoir of Madness* (New York: Random House, 1990), 78–79.

4. R. Huntley, "A Bridge of Faith," in *Walking in Two Worlds: Women's Spiritual Paths,"* ed. K. Vander Vort, J. H. Timmerman, and E. Lincoln (Saint Cloud, Minn.: North Star Press of Saint Cloud, 1991), 102–3.

5. J. Campbell, *The Hero with a Thousand Faces* (Princeton, N.J.: University Press, 1949).

6. S. M. Madigan, "Honoring the Void: Going Down and Moving Out. The Journey from Emptiness to Fullness," Theological Insights Program (Saint Paul, Minn.: The College of Saint Catherine, 1994).

7. T. Moore, *Care of the Soul* (New York: HarperCollins, 1992), 140–41.

8. C. McCarthy, *All the Pretty Horses* (New York: Random House, 1992), 235.

9. Z. N. Hurston, *Written by Herself*, ed. Jill K. Conway (New York: Vintage Books, 1992).

Appendix

1. F. Schatzberg and C. C. Nemeroff, *The American Psychiatric Press Textbook of Psychopharmacology* (Washington,

D.C.: American Psychiatric Press, 1995); *Physician's Desk Reference* (Montvale, N.J.: Medical Economics Company, 2000).

2. Ibid.

3. American Association of Hospital Pharmacists, *American Hospital Formulary Service Drug Information* (Bethesda, Md.: American Association of Hospital Pharmacists, 1993).

4. *Physician's Desk Reference* (Montvale, N.J.: Medical Economics Data, 1994), 764.

5. R. S. Schottenfeld, S. S. O'Malley, L. Smith, B. J. Rounsaville, and J. H. Jaffe, "Clinical Note: Limitation and Potential Hazards of MAOIs for the Treatment of Depressive Symptoms of Abstinent Alcoholics," *American Journal of Drug and Alcohol Abuse* 13, no. 3 (1989): 339–44; J. H. Jaffe, H. R. Kranzler, and D. A. Ciraulo, "Drugs Used in the Treatment of Alcoholism," in *Medical Diagnosis and Treatment of Alcoholism*, ed. J. H. Mendelson and N. K. Mello (New York: McGraw Hill, 1992), 421–61; R. Z. Litten and J. P. Allen, "Pharmacotherapy for Alcoholics with Collateral Depression or Anxiety: An Update of Research Findings" (forthcoming).

6. Ibid.

7. *Physician's Desk Reference* (2000), 2266. (See note 1, page 286.)

8. Schottenfeld et al., "Clinical Note"; Jaffe, Kranzler, Ciraulo, "Drugs Used in the Treatment of Alcoholism"; Litten and Allen, "Pharmacotherapy for Alcoholics." (See note 5.)

9. M. P. Freeman and A. L. Stoll, "Mood Stabilizer Combinations: A Review of Safety and Efficacy," *American Journal of Psychiatry* 155 (1998): 12–21.

10. Ibid.

11. Ibid.

12. Ibid.

Index

A

AA. *See* Alcoholics
Anonymous (AA)
*A.A. Member—Medications
and Other Drugs, The,* 185
AARP. *See* American
Association for Retired
People (AARP)
abuse, as cause of depression,
55, 58–59, 84
ACA. *See* Adult Children of
Alcoholics (ACA)
accelerated physical aging, 92
ACTH, 52
actions and behavior. *See* behavior and actions
addiction
and antidepressants,
191–201
and depression, 22–23,
26–30, 73–74, 195
See also recovery from
addiction

addictionologists, 195
adolescence, 27
Adult Children of Alcoholics
(ACA), 71, 189–90
affective disorders. *See* dysthymia; seasonal affective
disorder (SAD)
African Americans, 38
age, 39, 92, 211
AIDS, 74, 224
alcohol, 76, 173–74
alcoholic homes, 71–74, 81
Alcoholics Anonymous
(AA), 185–91, 193–95,
198, 244, 269
Alcoholics Anonymous, 269n
alcoholism, 152, 197–200.
See also addiction
ambivalence, 21
American Association for Retired People (AARP), 272
*American Journal of
Psychiatry,* 100–101

amines, 145, 146
amitriptyline hydrochloride.
   See Elavil
amotivational syndrome, 77
amoxapine. *See* Asendin
Amsterdam, 92
Andrews, Lewis, 239
Angelou, Maya, 223
anorexia. *See* eating disorders
Anorexia Nervosa and
   Related Eating Disorders,
   209
anticonvulsants, 153
antidepressant medications,
   143–212, 249–68
   AA encouragement,
      185–91
   and addiction, 191–201
   adjunct medications,
      208–9
   alcohol and drug use,
      173–74
   case studies, 153–66,
      169–72, 175–79, 185–96
   categories of, 144–53
   checklists for taking,
      143–44, 159–60, 172–73,
      201–2, 203–4
   CRF levels decreased with,
      53
   deciding to use, 153–60
   defined, 144
   discontinuing, 181–83
   dosage, 151, 206–8

future of, 183–84
herbal remedies, 183–84
long-term use, 174, 179–80
and pregnancy, 210–11,
   253, 268
and psychotherapy,
   100–101, 124–25
self-help, 201–2, 212
short-term use, 174–79
side effects, 151, 167–74,
   210
unique antidepressants,
   144, 152–53, 252–55
withdrawal, 181–83
See also monoamine oxi-
   dase inhibitors (MAOIs);
   mood stabilizers; selective serotonin re-uptake
   inhibitors (SSRIs); tricyclic antidepressants
anxiety, 20–21, 68, 209
anxiety-reducer substances,
   77
appetite, 9, 11. *See also* diet
   and nutrition
arteriosclerosis, 94
Asendin (amoxapine)
   dosage, 260
   how it works, 259
   side effects, 260
   as tricyclic, 147
assessment, in therapy, 99
associated causes or factors,
   63–78

Ativan, 77
Aventyl (nortriptyline hydrochloride)
dosage, 257
side effects, 257
as tricyclic, 147

B
barbiturates, 77
behavior and actions, 107–8, 111–12
biological causes or factors, 46–56, 72–74. *See also* family background
biorhythms, 55–56
bipolar depression, 15–17, 138–39, 153, 266
birth control pills, 64
blood pressure medications, 74–75, 84
brain chemistry. *See* chemical imbalances
Buchwald, Art, 35
bulimia. *See* eating disorders
bupropion hydrochloride. *See* Wellbutrin

C
Cade, John, 265
calming rituals, 140
Campbell, Joseph, 231
carbamazepine, 266–67. *See also* Tegretol
carbohydrates, 76, 137

careers, and depression, 40
Cavett, Dick, 36
CDC. *See* Centers for Disease Control (CDC)
Celexa (citalopram HBr)
dosage, 254
how it works, 254
side effects, 254
as SSRI, 149
Celtic religion, 232
Centers for Disease Control (CDC), 30, 87–88, 93
chat rooms. *See* Internet
chemical imbalances, 50–55, 75, 81–82, 199–200
chemical use, 78–79. *See also* alcohol; alcoholism
childhood experiences, 55, 56–58, 81, 83, 99, 237. *See also* family background
Chinese Americans, 38
circle of change, 100–112
citalopram HBr. *See* Celexa
cocaine, 77
cognitive-behavioral therapy, 100–112
Collins, Judy, 36
Columbia University, 93
concentration, lack of, 10
control, external locus of, 21
cortisol, 52
courage, 237–39, 247
CRF, 52–54

Cronkite, Kathy, 35
Cronkite, Walter, 35

D

death, and depression,
10–11, 87–96. *See also*
suicide
delusions, 14
Depakote (valproate)
  for bipolar illness, 266
  dosage, 267
  how it works, 267
  as mood stabilizer, 153,
    267–68
  use during pregnancy and
    nursing not recom-
    mended, 268
  side effects, 267
depression
  atypical, 12
  as bridge, not abyss,
    231–32, 247
  causes of, 45–86
  common threads of,
    20–21
  defined, 7
  as invisible, 1, 6
  lessons from/role of, 230
  and sobriety, 198–99
  statistics, 36–37, 41–42
  symptoms, 8–12
  as transformation, 232–33
  types of, 7–20
  typical, 12

  as visible, 42
  who has it, 35–43
depression spectrum disease,
  73
desipramine hydrochloride,
  208–9. *See also*
  Norpramin
despair, 106
Desyrel
  for insomnia, 209
  as unique/new, 152
diet and nutrition, 137–40,
  141. *See also* appetite
dietary supplements, 184
diltiazem, 267
distorted thinking, 14
doctors. *See* physicians
double depression, 14–15
doxepin hydrochloride. *See*
  Sinequan
drugs, effects on moods and
  states of mind, 76–77
dry drunk, 198
Duke University, 135, 184
dysthymia (mild depres-
  sion), 7, 13, 143, 224

E

eating disorders
  as cause of depression, 74,
    84
  use of Prozac, 209
  self-help, 84
  use of SSRIs, 152

eating right. *See* diet and
nutrition
educational backgrounds, 39
EEG. *See* electroencephalogram (EEG)
Effexor/Effexor XR
(venlafaxine)
dosage, 253
how it works, 253
use during pregnancy and
nursing not recom-
mended, 253
side effects, 253
as unique/new, 152
Elavil (amitriptyline
hydrochloride)
dosage, 256
how it works, 256
side effects, 256
as tricyclic, 147
elderly, 39, 211
electroconvulsant/electro-
shock therapy, CRF levels
decreased with, 53
electroencephalogram
(EEG), 55
Emory University, 53
emotional abuse, as cause of
depression, 58–59
emotions. *See* feelings
Emotions Anonymous, 244
emptiness, 106
endogenous depression,
18–19

environmental causes or factors, 56–59, 71–72, 74
ethnicity, 38–39
exercise and physical activity, 135–36, 139, 141
external locus of control,
21

F
family
giving support to, 217–20
receiving support from,
213–17, 220–21
relationships with, 131–32
self-help, 222
family background
alcoholic homes, 71–74
genetics, 46–50, 73–74,
80–81, 83
See also alcoholic homes;
childhood experiences
fatigue, 10
feelings, 105–7, 110–11. *See
also* emotional abuse
Feminine Face of God, The,
226–27
flight or fight response, 51
fluoxetine hydrochloride.
See Prozac
folic acid deficiency, 138
food. *See* diet and nutrition;
eating disorders
friends
giving support to, 217–20

receiving support from, 213–17, 220–22
relationships with, 131–32
self-help, 222

G
gender, as factor in depression, 78. *See also* women
genetics. *See* family background
Glasser, William, 111
Greden, John, 179–80
grief, 5, 99. *See also* losses
guilt, feelings of, 10

H
Halcion, 77
hallucinations, 14
H.A.L.T., 198
Hatsukami, Dorothy, 202–3
health care costs, 40
helplessness, learned, as cause of depression, 61–63
hepatitis C, 74
herbal remedies, 183–84
Higher Power, 195, 225–26
hopelessness
   and eating disorders, 74
   and nicotine addiction, 68, 71
   and suicide, 6
hormonal fluctuations, 63–68, 76, 84–85
hot lines, 125

HPA axis. *See* hypothalamic-pituitary-adrenal (HPA) axis
human race, connection to, 235–36
Huntley, Rose, 231
Hurston, Zora Neale, 238
Hypericum perforatum. *See* St. John's Wort
hypomanic state, 2, 16
hypothalamic-pituitary-adrenal (HPA) axis, 51–54, 56, 94
hypothyroidism, 63–64

I
iatrogenic depression, 74–75
imipramine. *See* Tofranil
inadequacy, 106
income levels, 37–38
indecisiveness, 20–21
insomnia. *See* sleeping problems
interferon, 74
International Society of Sports Psychology, 135
Internet, 1–2, 3
irritability, 106
isocarboxazid. *See* Marplan
isolation, 21, 58

J
Jewish population, 38–39
Journal of Family Practice, 70

K
Konner, Melvin, 160–61
Korean Americans, 38
Kramer, Peter, 213

L
Latinos, 38
Lewis, J. M., 128, 129
lifestyle, and recovery from
   depression, 127–41. *See
   also* relationships
light and sunlight, need for.
   See seasonal affective disorder (SAD)
Listening to Prozac (Kramer),
   213
lithium (lithium salts)
 use by alcoholics/addicts,
   266–67
 for bipolar illness, 153, 266
 dosage, 265–66
 how it works, 265
 for manic episodes, 265
 as mood stabilizer, 153,
   265–67
 side effects, 265
 and valproate, 266
Lithobid, 265
living in the moment,
   236–37
loneliness, 21, 58
losses, as cause of depression,
   5, 60–61, 83. *See also*
   grief

Ludiomil (maprotiline
   hydrochloride), 259
Luvox
 as SSRI, 149
 withdrawal symptoms,
   182–83

M
Madigan, Shawn, 232
major depression. *See* major
   depressive episodes
major depressive episodes
 atypical symptoms, 11
 defined, 7–8
 symptoms, 8–12
manic-depressive illness,
   15–17, 41
MAO. *See* monoamine oxi-
   dase (MAO)
MAOIs. *See* monoamine oxidase inhibitors (MAOIs)
maprotiline hydrochloride.
   See Ludiomil
marijuana, 77
marital status, 39–40,
   129–31
Marplan (isocarboxazid)
 use by alcoholics/addicts,
   262
 dosage, 262
 how it works, 261
 as MAOI, 145
 side effects, 262
Mayo Clinic, 93–94

medical costs, 40
medications
  as cause of depression,
    74–75, 84
  and psychotherapy, 124–25
  as treatment for depres-
    sion, 249–68
  See also antidepressant
    medications; anxiety-
    reducer substances
melatonin, 76
menopause, 67–68, 85
menstrual cycles, 64–68.
  See also premenstrual
    syndrome (PMS)
mild depression. *See*
  dysthymia
mirtazapine. *See* Remeron
moments, importance of,
  236–37
monoamine oxidase (MAO),
  145
monoamine oxidase in-
  hibitors (MAOIs)
  antidepressants, 144–47,
    261–65
  dietary restrictions, 201
mood disorder, 13
mood stabilizers, 144, 153,
  265–68
moods and moodiness, 8
Moore, Thomas, 233
Morita therapy, 56
mortality. *See* death

N
NAMI. *See* National Alliance
  for the Mentally Ill
  (NAMI)
Nardil (phenelzine sulfate)
  use by alcoholics/addicts,
    263
  dosage, 263
  how it works, 262–63
  as MAOI, 145
  side effects, 263
National Alliance for the
  Mentally Ill (NAMI),
  125, 272
National Depressive and
  Manic-Depressive Asso-
  ciation (NDMDA), 271
National Foundation for De-
  pressive Illness, Inc., 272
National Health and
  Nutrition Epidemiologi-
  cal Study, 93
National Institute of Mental
  Health (NIMH), 73, 134,
  184, 271
National Institutes of
  Health, 134
NDMDA. *See* National
  Depressive and Manic-
  Depressive Association
  (NDMDA)
nefazodone. *See* Serzone
negative evaluations, 103–4
neglect, 55

neurochemistry, 145–46
neurons, 148
neurotransmitters
　discussed, 50–51
　and hormones, 63, 76
　MAOIs, 146
　tricyclics, 148
　unique/new anti-
　　depressants, 152
New York Times Magazine,
　The, 160–61
nicotine addiction, 68–71, 79
nifedipine, 267
NIMH. *See* National
　Institute of Mental
　Health (NIMH)
norepinephrine, 50–51
Norpramin (desipramine
　hydrochloride)
　dosage, 258
　how it works, 257
　side effects, 257
　as tricyclic, 147
nortriptyline hydrochloride.
　See Aventyl; Pamelor
nutrition. *See* diet and
　nutrition

O
OA. *See* Overeaters
　Anonymous (OA)
obsession, 20–21
obsessive-compulsive dis-
　order, use of SSRIs, 152

Oliver, Mary, 97
omega-3 fats, 138–39
one day at a time, 236–37
opiates, 77
optimism, learned,
　132–33
oral contraceptives, 64
overcompensation, 21
OvereatersAnonymous
　(OA), 189–90

P
painkillers, 77
Pamelor (nortriptyline hydro-
　chloride), 257
panic disorder, use of SSRIs,
　152
Parnate (tranylcypromine
　sulfate)
　use by alcoholics/addicts,
　　264–65
　dosage, 264
　how it works, 263–64
　as MAOI, 145
　side effects, 264
paroxetine, sexual func-
　tioning side effects, 151.
　See also Paxil
'Pass It On,' 188
Paxil (paroxetine)
　case study, 176
　dosage, 251
　how it works, 251
　side effects, 251

as SSRI, 149
withdrawal symptoms, 182
PDR. *See Physician's Desk Reference* (PDR)
Pepper, Bert, 175
perimenopause, 67, 85
phenelzine sulfate. *See* Nardil
physical abuse, as cause of depression, 58–59
physicians, 195–96
Physician's Desk Reference (PDR), 261, 264–65
PMS. *See* premenstrual syndrome (PMS)
postpartum depression, 64–65
post-traumatic stress disorder (PTSD), 58–59
pregnancy, and medications, 210–11, 253, 268. *See also* postpartum depression
premenstrual dysphoric disorder, 65–66
premenstrual syndrome (PMS), 65–66, 85, 211
primary depression, 26–28
Prozac (fluoxetine hydrochloride)
for addiction, 200
dosage, 150
for eating disorders, 209
how it works, 249–50

side effects, 250
as SSRI, 149
withdrawal symptoms, 182–83
psychoanalytic theory, 57
psychotherapy, 97–125
action phase, 119
and antidepressants, 100–101, 124–25
assessment, 99
contemplation phase, 118
defined, 98–100
maintenance phase, 119–20
and medications, 124–25
patterns of change in therapy, 117–20, *120*
precontemplation phase, 118
preparation phase, 118
and recovery from addiction, 121–22
self-help, 125
time frame, 122–23
topics, 98–99
See also cognitive-behavioral therapy
psychotic features, 14
PTSD. *See* post-traumatic stress disorder (PTSD)

R
Random Acts of Kindness, 112
rapid cyclers, 15

rapid eye movement (REM), 55

reactive depression, 19–20

rebellion, during adolescence, 27

recovery from addiction, 3
  antidepressants, 185–201
  case studies, 24–25
  death and suicide, 94–95
  depression, 3, 22–25, 40–41, 43, 86, 121–22
  depression, causes of, 78–79, 86
  mental health professionals, 34
  psychotherapy, 121–22
  spirituality, 239–45, 247–48

relapse, to chemical use, 121–22

relationships, 39–40, 99. 127–32. *See also* family. friends

REM. *See* rapid eye movement (REM)

Remeron (mirtazapine)
  dosage, 255
  how it works, 255
  reduced sexual side effects, 151, 152–53
  side effects, 151, 152–53, 255
  as unique/new, 152–53

residuals of depression, 101

Rothko, Mark, 35–36

Rubel, Juean, 209

S

sacred spaces, 232

SAD. *See* seasonal affective disorder (SAD)

S-adenosylmethionine (SAM-e), 138, 184

SAM-e. *See* S-adenosylmethionine (SAM-e)

SA\VE (Suicide Awareness\Voices of Education), 271

schedules and scheduling, as lifestyle help, 140, 141

seasonal affective disorder (SAD), 17, 76, 85, 133–34, 176

secondary depression, 28–29

selective serotonin re-uptake inhibitors (SSRIs)
  adjuncts to, 208–9
  antidepressants, 144, 149–52, 249–51
  sexual side effects, 151, 152–53, 210
  withdrawal or discontinuation syndrome, 181–83

self-concept, 135

self-doubt, 21

self-esteem, 58, 135, 175

self-help, 4
  antidepressants, 201–2, 212

depression, 33–34, 42–43
depression, causes of,
    82–86
  family and friends, 222
  lifestyle, 140–41
  psychotherapy, 125
  spirituality, 246–48
  suicide, 89–91, 95–96
self-worth, 61–63, 74. *See
    also* worthlessness
Seligman, Martin, 132
serotonin
  discussed, 50–51
  folic acid deficiency, 138
  genetics, 74
  mood regulator, 138
  seasonal affective disorder,
    76
  See also selective serotonin
    re-uptake inhibitors
    (SSRIs)
serotonin re-uptake in-
    hibitors. *See* selective
    serotonin re-uptake
    inhibitors (SSRIs)
sertraline hydrochloride. *See*
    Zoloft
Serzone (nefazodone)
  dosage, 254
  how it works, 253
  reduced sexual side effects,
    151, 152–53
  side effects, 151, 152–53,
    254

and unique/new, 153
sexual abuse, as cause of
    depression, 58–59
sexual side effects of
    medications
  antidepressants, 160, 167,
    210
  Asendin (amoxapine), 260
  dosage reduction, 151
  paroxetine, 151
  Remeron, 151, 152–53
  Serzone, 151, 152–53
  SSRIs, 151, 152–53, 210
  tricyclics, 148–49
  Wellbutrin, 151, 152–53
shame, 74, 218
Sinequan (doxepin
    hydrochloride)
  dosage, 258–59
  how it works, 258
  side effects, 258
  as tricyclic, 147
sleep cycles, 55–56. *See also*
    sleeping problems
sleeping pills, 77, 85
sleeping problems, 9, 11,
    169, 209, 210
sobriety, and resolution of
    depression, 198–99
social phobia, 20–21
somatic complaints, of older
    adults, 39
Southeast Asian refugees,
    38

spiritual crisis, vs. major depression, 229–30
spirituality, 223–48
  asking spiritual questions, 224–26
  depression as spiritual phenomenon, 223–24
  images of depression, 230–33
  messages of depression, 233–39
  recognizing role of depression, 230
  recovery from addiction, 239–45
  self-help, 246–48
  when to get help, 226–30
SSRIs. *See* selective serotonin re-uptake inhibitors (SSRIs)
St. John of the Cross, 225–26
St. John's Wort (Hypericum perforatum), 183–84
statistics
  depression, 36–37, 41–42
  suicide, 30, 87–88
stigma, 218
stimulants, 77
stress, 99
Styron, William, 36, 87, 216–17, 228–29
suicide
  and depression, 87–91
  and hopelessness, 6

self-help, 89–91, 95–96
statistics, 30, 87–88
thoughts of, 10–11
warning signs, 88–89
Suicide Awareness\Voices of Education (SA\VE), 271
sunlight, need for. *See* seasonal affective disorder (SAD)
synapse, 50, 146
Synthroid (thyroid hormone), 209

T
Tegretol (carbamazepine)
  dosage, 268
  how it works, 268
  as mood stabilizer, 153
  side effects, 268
therapists, locating, 112–16
therapy. *See* psychotherapy
thinking, 103–5, 109–10
thoughts-feelings-behavior, balance of, 101–3, 105, 107–9, 122
Tiebout, Harry, 188
Tofranil (imipramine)
  dosage, 256
  how it works, 255
  side effects, 255–56
  as tricyclic, 147
tranquilizers, 77, 85

tranylcypromine sulfate. *See*
    Parnate
trauma, as cause of depression, 59–60, 237
traumatic brain injury, 75
trazodone, 152, 252. *See also*
    Desyrel
tricyclic antidepressants,
    144, 147–49, 208–9,
    255–61
tryptophan deficiency, 137
tuberculosis, 145
Twelve Step programs,
    188–90, 194–95, 226,
    244–45, 248
Twelve Steps, 239–44, 247,
    269
twins, 47–48
tyramine, 146–47

U
uncertainty, 21
University of California, San
    Diego, 133
University of California,
    San Francisco, Department of Psychiatry,
    69–70
University of Houston, 117
University of Pennsylvania,
    100–101
University of Rhode Island,
    117
uppers, 144

V
Valliant, George, 92
valproate, 266. *See also*
    Depakote
values, changing, 234–35
vegetative symptoms, 12
venlafaxine. *See* Effexor
verapamil, 267
Vestra, 152
Veterans Administration
    (U.S.), 23
vulnerability, 78–79, 237

W
Wehr, Thomas, 134
Wellbutrin (bupropion
    hydrochloride)
    use by alcoholics/addicts,
        261
    dosage, 261
    how it works, 260
    reduced sexual side effects,
        151, 152–53
    side effects, 260–61
    as unique/new, 152
Wilson, Bill, 188
Wing, Nell, 188
women, and depression, 37,
    64–68, 78, 84–85, 128.
    See also menstrual cycles;
    postpartum depression
worry, 20–21
worthlessness, feelings of, 10,
    107. *See also* self-worth

X
Xanax
  as addictive, 210
  as depressant, 77
  not recommended for sleep
    problems, 210

Z
Zoloft (sertraline
  hydrochloride)

and addiction, 192
case study, 176, 192
dosage, 251
how it works, 250
research study, 135
side effects, 250
as SSRI, 149
withdrawal symptoms,
  182–83

About the Author

Patricia L. Owen is executive vice president for research at Hazelden and directs the Butler Center for Research at Hazelden. She holds her doctoral degree in adult clinical psychology and obtained a master's degree in health care administration, both from the University of Minnesota. Dr. Owen has published numerous articles on alcohol and drug problems and has given many presentations at national conferences.

HAZELDEN INFORMATION AND EDUCATIONAL SERVICES is a division of the Hazelden Foundation, a not-for-profit organization. Since 1949, Hazelden has been a leader in promoting the dignity and treatment of people afflicted with the disease of chemical dependency.

The mission of the foundation is to improve the quality of life for individuals, families, and communities by providing a national continuum of information, education, and recovery services that are widely accessible; to advance the field through research and training; and to improve our quality and effectiveness through continuous improvement and innovation.

Stemming from that, the mission of this division is to provide quality information and support to people wherever they may be in their personal journey—from education and early intervention, through treatment and recovery, to personal and spiritual growth.

Although our treatment programs do not necessarily use everything Hazelden publishes, our bibliotherapeutic materials support our mission and the Twelve Step philosophy upon which it is based. We encourage your comments and feedback.

The headquarters of the Hazelden Foundation are in Center City, Minnesota. Additional treatment facilities are located in Chicago, Illinois; New York, New York; Plymouth, Minnesota; St. Paul, Minnesota; and West Palm Beach, Florida. At these sites, we provide a continuum of care for men and women of all ages. Our Plymouth facility is designed specifically for youth and families.

For more information on Hazelden, please call **1-800-257-7800**. Or you may access our World Wide Web site on the Internet at **www.hazelden.org**.